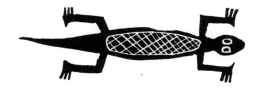

PAN-AFRICANISM
For Beginners

Written by: Sid Lemelle

Illustration and Design: Ife Nii owoo

Writers and Readers

New York, London

Writers and Readers Publishing, Incorporated
P.O. Box 461, Village Station
New York, NY 10014
c/o Airlift Book Company
26 Eden Grove
London, N7 8EF
England

Text Copyright © Sid Lemelle
Illustrations © Ife Nii Owoo
Cover Design: Ife Nii Owoo

A Writers and Readers Documentary Comic Book
Copyright © 1992
Library of Congress Catalog Card Number: 91-050561
ISBN # Trade: 0-86316-148-0
1 2 3 4 5 6 7 8 9 0

Manufactured in the United States of America

Beginners Documentary Comic Books are published by Writers and Readers Publishing, Inc. Its trademark, consisting of the words "For Beginners, Writers and Readers Documentary Comic Books" and Writers and Readers logo, is registered in the U.S. Patent and Trademark Office and in other countries.

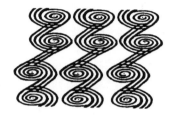

PAN-AFRICANISM
for beginners

ACKNOWLEDGMENTS

My thanks to Ruth Wilson Gilmore, Craig Gilmore, Glenn Thompson, Patricia Karimi Taleghani, Robin D.G. Kelley, Diedra Harris-Kelley, Theresa Bishop, Elaine Price, Bryant Lemelle, Earl Philips, Jojo Kumankumah.

This book is dedicated to the memory of my parents, Sostan and Emma Lemelle, whose love and wisdom hepled guide me through life and to my father-in-Law, Mzee Mohammed bin Salum Khaleff, a wise and gentle man and to my Pan-African family in Los Angeles, New Orleans and Dar es Salaam:

Salima Mohammed Lemelle, Sean Lemelle,Sabra Hall, Ibrahim Dhalla, Salim Lemelle, Herbert Lemelle, Leah Lemelle, Dolores Moore, Meryl Bishop, Mildred Lemelle, James Dodson, Barbara Bair, Bibi Rahia Seif and Rahma Khaleff for for their Love and support.

Sid Lemelle

PREFACE

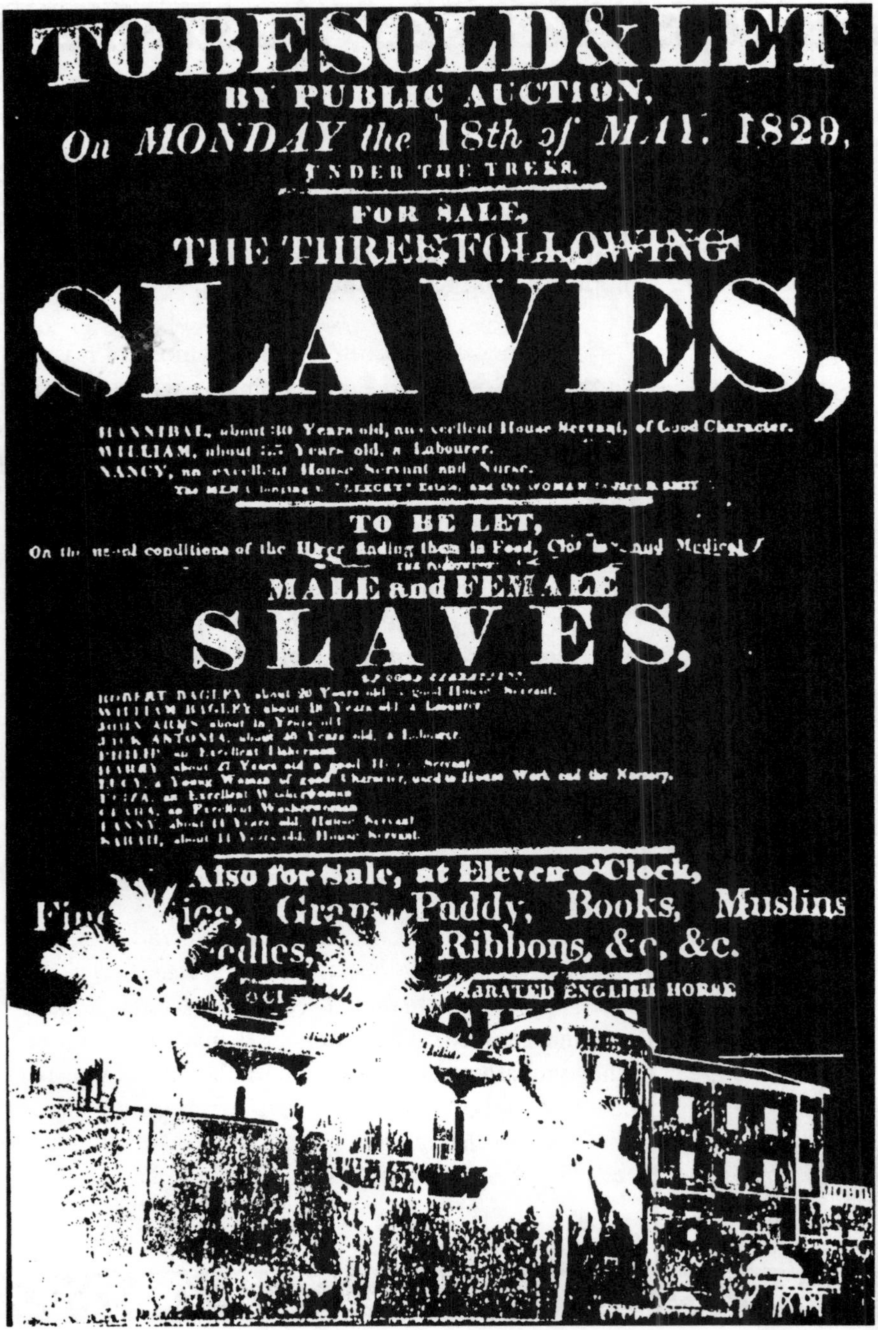
TO BE SOLD & LET
BY PUBLIC AUCTION,
On MONDAY the 18th of MAY, 1829,
FOR SALE,
SLAVES,
TO BE LET,
MALE and FEMALE
SLAVES,
Also for Sale, at Eleven o'Clock,
Paddy, Books, Muslins
Ribbons, &c. &c.

The idea for this book began many years ago. You might say that it took me twenty years to figure out what exactly Pan-Africanism is all about. But only after completing the work have I begun to really understand. Possibly the reason is that Pan-Africanism has a two hundred year history, incorporating thousands of people and hundreds of organizations. Likewise the idea of Pan-Africanism has meant so many different things to so many different people. Anyway, writing a "popular" history of such a complex and misunderstood idea has been challenging —to say the least. Now that I've gotten the disclaimer out of the way, I feel the need to clarify several other points.

Any attempt to write a "readable" work on Pan-Africanism raises the problems of terms. A few scholars (fortunately only a few) have seen fit to make a distinction between what they believe are two different categories of Pan-Africanism. According to them, the first category is "organized" Pan-Africanism (spelled with a capital "P"); that is, those attempts to create a social movement and an international (dues paying) organization which would further the cause of Black people around the world. The second form of Pan-Africanism (often spelled with a small "p") is "unorganized" (not messy or confused, just unorganized). This category is made up of those who sympathize and identify with the African heritage and support the aims of Pan-Africanism. Likewise, some scholars distinguish between what they call "Pan-Negroism" (i.e. a narrow understanding of

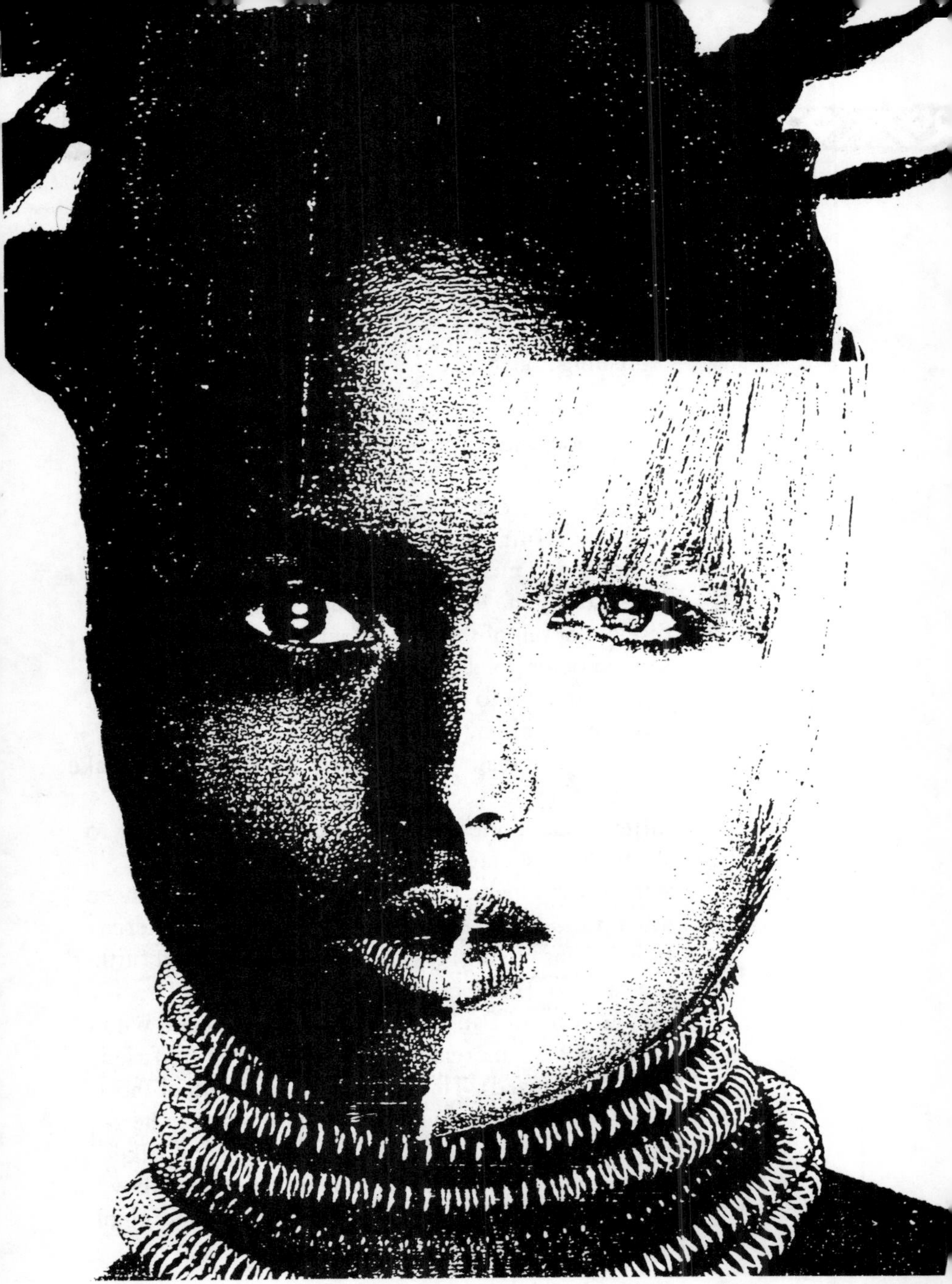

Pan-Africanism based simply on race), "Proto-Pan-Africanism," and Pan-Africanism (with a capital "P"). With all due respect to my distinguished and distinguishing colleagues, I will not make such distinctions. For the average reader it seems counterproductive and confusing to make distinctions between the sentiments and ideas of Pan-Africanism and the movement itself–in fact, such distinctions hide some very important class and ethnic contradictions (which I promise to clear up in the text).

The second point of clarification has to do with nomenclature, especially the terms "Black," "Afro-American," "African-American." Which ones to use, which ones to avoid? (Notice I left out "Negro" and "colored," which I all but eliminated from my vocabulary in the sixties). This is an old debate, dating back to the 18th century. I use the inclusive term "Black" to include all people of African descent. Likewise I use "people of color"–not colored people– to include peasant and working-class people of Africa, Asia, Latin America and the Caribbean. Also the narrower "diasporan" to include all people of African descent in the "new world." "Afro-[short for African, not the comb or hairdo] American" and "African-American" are used to specify a particular group. I use the terms interchangeably depending on the context and emphasis.

Now, if all this has not confused you to the point where you have decided not to read the book, I (and my publisher) encourage you to jump into the text.

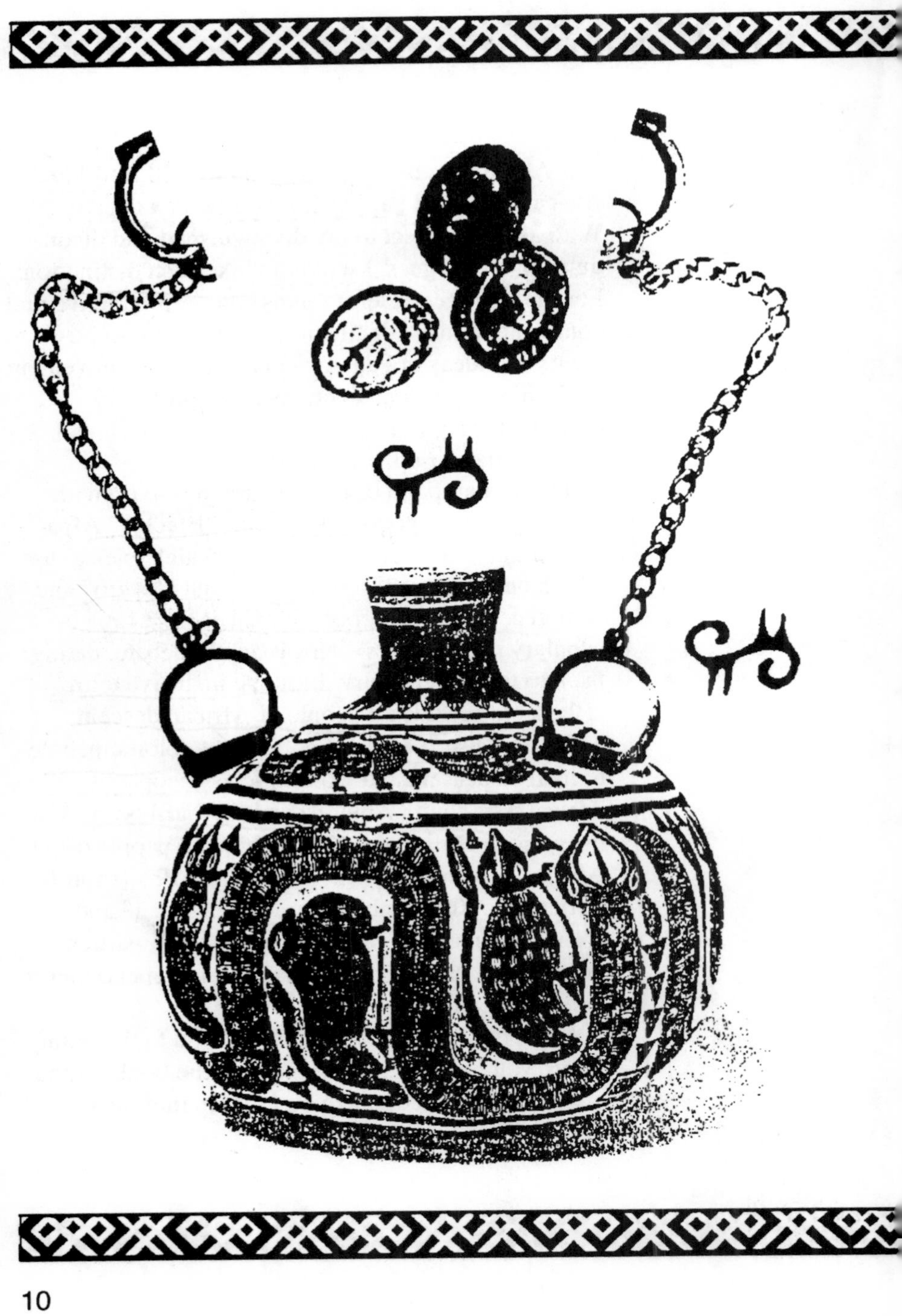

Pan-Africanism

is a simple yet complex concept.
Essentially, it is a set of ideas
and ideologies containing social
and cultural, political and
economic, material and spiritual
aspects.

"Pan"

means all; so Pan-Africanism
includes all people of African
ancestry living in continental
Africa and throughout the world.

*T*HE AFRICAN "DIASPORA."

Pan-Africanism tries to create a bond between Black people of Africa and the Diaspora, recognizing that they are all linked to Africa through a common experience of oppression and slavery.

The Pan-African idea and movement grew out of Black people's desire to rediscover and recover their identity and heritage and to fight for their liberation from colonialism and racism.

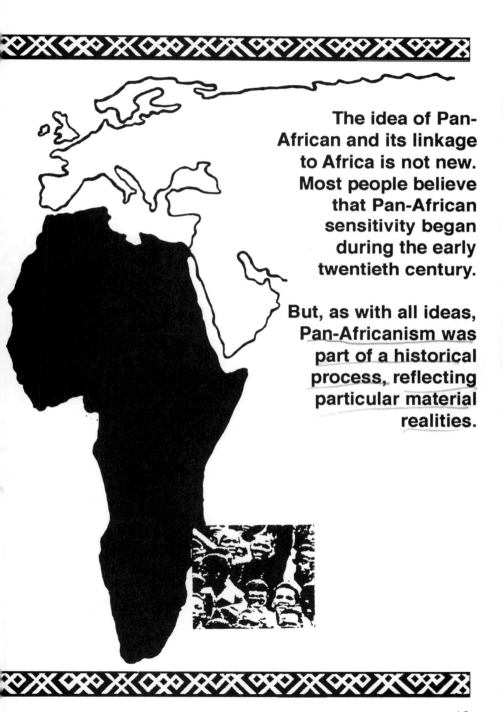

The idea of Pan-African and its linkage to Africa is not new. Most people believe that Pan-African sensitivity began during the early twentieth century.

But, as with all ideas, Pan-Africanism was part of a historical process, reflecting particular material realities.

Thus, long before the organized movement arose, the suffering and degradation of Africans and their descendants brought forth Pan-Africanism. The struggle actually began when the Portuguese adventurer Antam Goncalvez took twelve Africans from the continent as slave laborers in 1441.

It continued for the next 400 years as White masters, fearing revolts, subjected African slaves to cruel and inhumane treatment.

During the so-called "seasoning process," slave overseers tried to "break" the Africans' spirit. They tried to make them into submissive American slaves. Slave masters believed that if they took away the Africans' language, customs, names and, above all, their history, slaves would forget their African cultural heritage. Without a heritage, the planter class thought they could easily control slaves and made them accept their slave status.

Historically, Pan-Africanism has had a strong cultural orientation. Pan-Africanists believed that if Black people could regain a sense of pride in their history and heritage, they would then fight for their freedom.

Thus the initial thrust of the movement was to restore Black people's cultural identity by glorifying the African past: the history of great kingdoms, wise rulers and untold wealth. Pan-Africanist praised the kingdoms of

Western Sudan: Ghana, Mali and Songhai, wise rulers like Mansa Musa (1312-1337), Sonni Ali (1464-1492) and Askia Mohammad (1493-1529), and the wealth of Ancient Egypt and Mwana Matapa.

EMPIRE OF GHANA
(c. 350 - 1076 A.D.)

MANDINGO EMPIRE
(c. 850 - 1433 A.D.)
&
SONGHAI EMPIRE
(c. 690 - 1? & 1468 - 1591 A.D.)

Timbuktu   Gao

Niger R.

Lake Chad

N

Throughout the history of slavery in the Americas, Africans fought to maintain their identity and dignity. Pan-Africanism is rooted in that struggle.

Out of the cultural ideas associated with Pan-Africanism, a political movement emerged in the 20th century. Many Black people organized political groups, and ultimately a movement, fighting for economic, political and human rights.

Yet this struggle was not without contradictions. Over the years, Africans and their descendants have found themselves in many different societies and cultures — from Harlem to Haiti, from Brixton to Soweto. They spoke different languages, had different class, gender and religious orientations. Out of these differences grew divergent ideas and forms of Pan-Africanism. In turn, these differences caused confusion about the aims, tactics and usefulness of the idea. Indeed, some critics doubted the very existence of the term. At times, Pan-Africanism was used interchangeably (although mistakenly) with such concepts as AFRICAN PERSONALITY, AFRICAN NATIONALISM, BLACK NATIONALISM, AFRICAN SOCIALISM, NEGRITUDE, BLACK POWER, etc.

This book tells the story of Pan-Africanism by looking at the struggle of Black people for dignity and self- determination. It examines the often contradictory development of Pan-Africanism as an idea, an ideology and a movement. Obviously, we cannot cover all the individuals, organizations and ideas that make up Pan-Africanism. As much as possible, we will concentrate on the most salient aspects of the historical struggle.

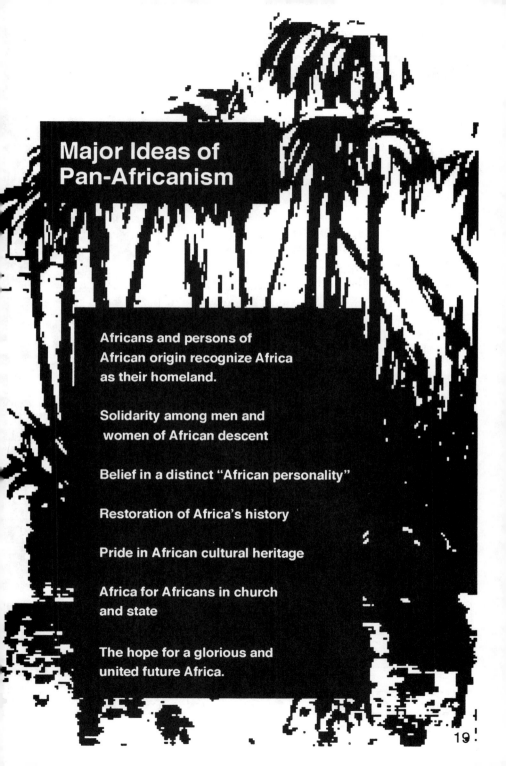

Major Ideas of Pan-Africanism

Africans and persons of
African origin recognize Africa
as their homeland.

Solidarity among men and
women of African descent

Belief in a distinct "African personality"

Restoration of Africa's history

Pride in African cultural heritage

Africa for Africans in church
and state

The hope for a glorious and
united future Africa.

We will never know the exact year the term "**Pan-African**" was first used. Nor will we ever discover the name of the person who first expressed the sentiment of Pan-Africanism. We do know that it started in the so-called "New World," probably in the 18th century. We are also fairly certain that it was a reaction to the oppression of black people and the racist practices common in the slave era.

TO BE SOLD on board the Ship *Bance: Ifland*, on tuefday the 6th of *May* next, at *Afhley-Ferry*; a choice cargo of about 250 fine healthy

NEGROES,

juft arrived from the Windward & Rice Coaft. —The utmoft care has already been taken, and fhall be continued, to keep them free from the leaft danger of being infected with the SMALL-POX, no boat having been board, and all other communication w people from *Charles-Town* prevented.

Auftin, Laurens, & Appleby.

N. B. Full one Half of the above Negroes have had SMALL-POX in their own Country.

In both the West Indies and United States, slave societies denied African descendents their basic human rights.

From earliest times, slaves rebelled against the "peculiar institution" of slavery, and many lost their lives — but still the misery continued. Some Black people (both slave and so-called "free Blacks") considered returning to Africa as the only way to escape their humiliating lives in slave society. For them, Africa was home.

One such person was **PRINCE HALL** (1735-1807), a Boston minister and African Freemason Grand Master. In 1787, ten years after arriving from Barbados, Hall petitioned the Massachusetts Legislative Assembly for help in returning poor Blacks to their African homeland. Not surprisingly, they ignored Hall's request.

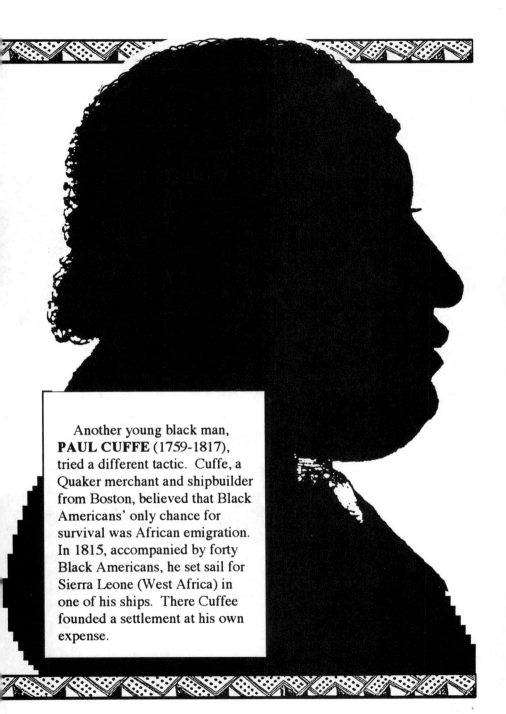

Another young black man, **PAUL CUFFE** (1759-1817), tried a different tactic. Cuffe, a Quaker merchant and shipbuilder from Boston, believed that Black Americans' only chance for survival was African emigration. In 1815, accompanied by forty Black Americans, he set sail for Sierra Leone (West Africa) in one of his ships. There Cuffee founded a settlement at his own expense.

Not all African Americans shared Hall's and Cuffee's views on emigration.

In 1816, White American "liberals" founded the **AMERICAN COLONIZA-TION SOCIETY (ACS).** The organization's main purpose was to finance and arrange for the removal of **"free Blacks"** to Africa (Liberia).

However, groups like the **ANNUAL CONVENTION OF THE FREE COL-ORED PEOPLE** and individuals like

DR. MARTIN R. DELANY
(1812-1885) [who later changed his attitude] and...

FREDERICK DOUGLASS

(1817-1895) argued against emigration. They believed that the ACS was a conspiracy to deny Blacks their rights. They felt that the United States was their home, and that they should remain.

The issue of repatriation/ emigration split many 19th century northern "free Black" communities — a debate which continued into the 20th century.

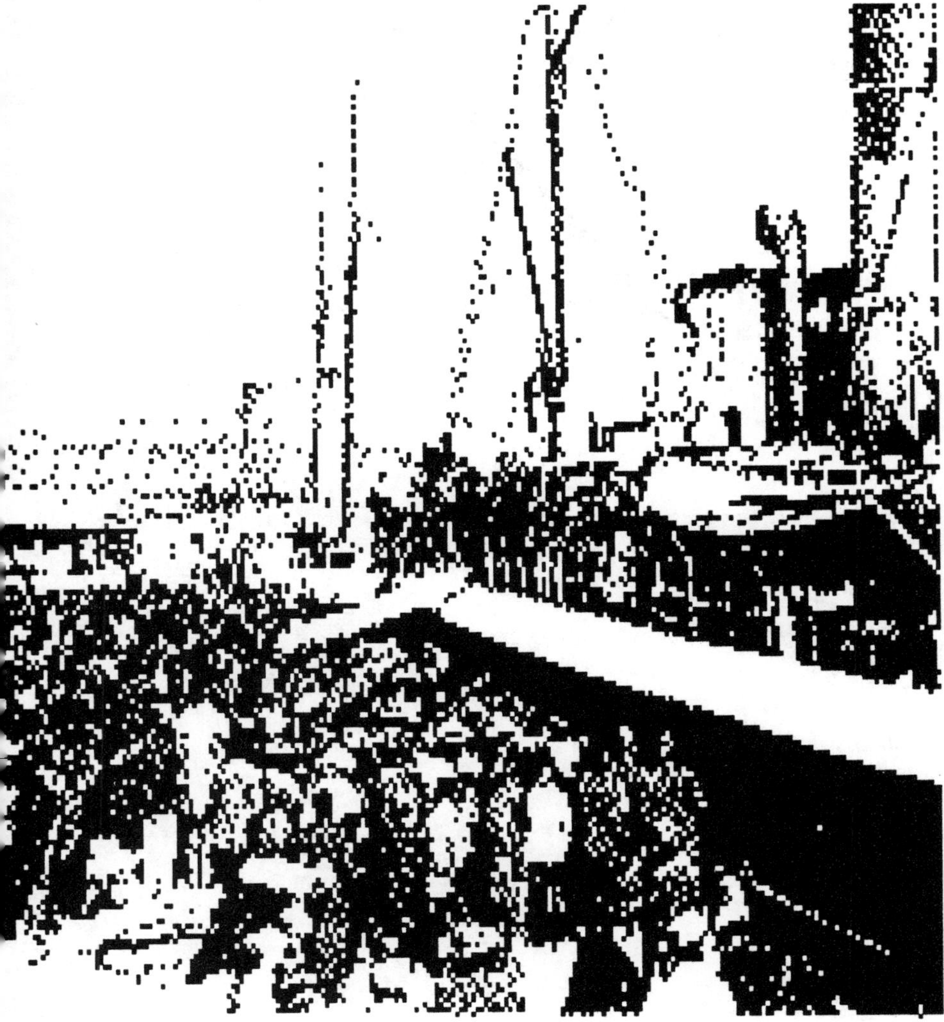

SIERRA LEONE:

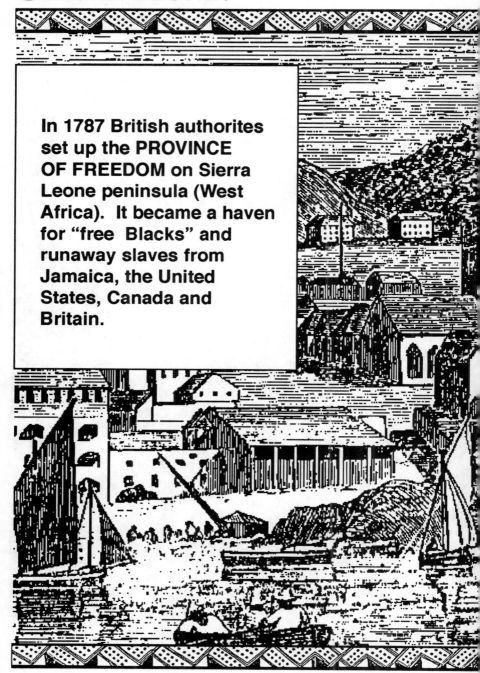

In 1787 British authorites set up the PROVINCE OF FREEDOM on Sierra Leone peninsula (West Africa). It became a haven for "free Blacks" and runaway slaves from Jamaica, the United States, Canada and Britain.

INDEPENDENCE 1961

10/-

SIERRA LEONE

The Sierra Leone Company, which ran the province, included British businessmen interested in developing trade and **"free labor"** [meaning **"free"** to be exploited]. Also, after the abolition of the slave trade in 1807, the British Anti-Slavery Squadron rescued Africans from slave ships and returned them to Sierra Leone's capital, Freetown. The local Yoruba people called these returnees **"Saros."**

However, the company treated them like slaves, which they resisted. Eventually the British state took control, and Sierra Leone later became a colony.

*L*IBERIA:

Several hundred miles
to the south of Sierra Leone;
a similar ex-slave community

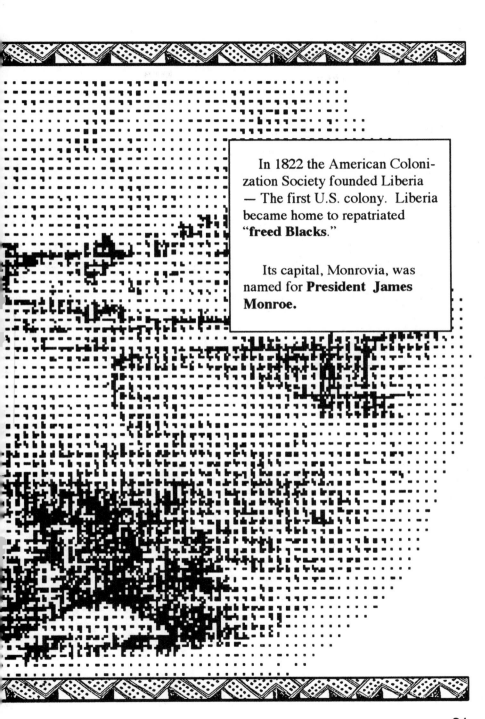

In 1822 the American Colonization Society founded Liberia — The first U.S. colony. Liberia became home to repatriated **"freed Blacks."**

Its capital, Monrovia, was named for **President James Monroe.**

Repatriation to Africa also had supporters among African descendants in the West Indies. Probably the best example was...

OLAUDAH EQUIANO:

(1745-1801),

or **GUSTAVUS VASSA** the African, as he was later known. Slave raiders kidnapped the young Vassa from his home in Nigeria and sold him into slavery in the West Indies. He bought his freedom years later and headed for England. There Equiano published a famous autobiography which praised the integrity and intelligence of African peoples. He also advocated returning to the motherland. Around 1792 he helped several freed African slaves go to Sierra Leone, although he himself was never able to return.

I don't know bout you,but I eady to get the ell otta here nd go back to .frica "

Returning to Africa also interested other West Indians and Latin American Blacks.

The Jamaican-born journalist **JOHN B. RUSSWURM** (1799-1851) became a strong supporter of repatriation. Although at first skeptical about returning to Africa, he eventually changed his mind. In 1830 Russwurm went to Liberia and founded a newspaper, the Liberia Herald.

In 1897, another West Indian, **Dr. ALBERT THRONE**, formed the AFRICAN COLONIAL ENTERPRISE to relocate African descendents to Africa.

Also, Latin American Blacks (particularly from Brazil) returned to Africa. In Dahomey and Nigeria they were called **AMARO**.

The Idea Takes Shape

An added factor which gave rise to Pan-African consciousness was the doctrine of White Supremacy. Many Whites believed that they were innately superior to people with darker skins. One such racist argument, Social Darwinism, was revived.

My Head's the biggest because I'm superior

IRISH IBERIAN.

ANGLO-TEUTONIC.

NEGRO.

7"

8"

6"

In the mid-19th century, a new, supposedly "scientific" racism began to spread. It was based on a distorted understanding of the **Charles Darwin** (1809-1882) "survival of fittest" theory.

Supporters of so-called **Social Darwinism** saw his theory as the key to human evolution and, as we will see, a justification for colonial exploitation.

According to this theory, Africans and other people of color were in the lowest rank on the human pecking order (fit only for rule by their White superiors).

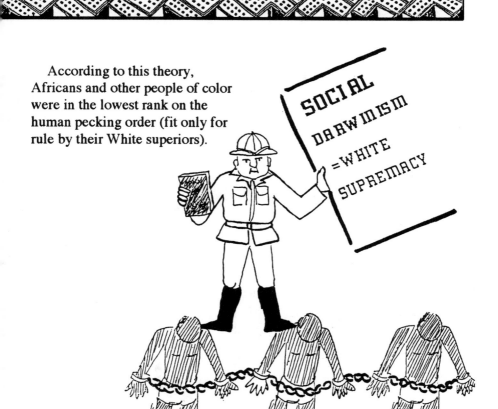

SOCIAL DARWINISM =WHITE SUPREMACY

White colonists believed themselves to be racially and culturally superior to people of color. Thus, they were able to view themselves as the providers of "civilization" to Africans rather than the economic exploiters they really were.

Defending the African Heritage

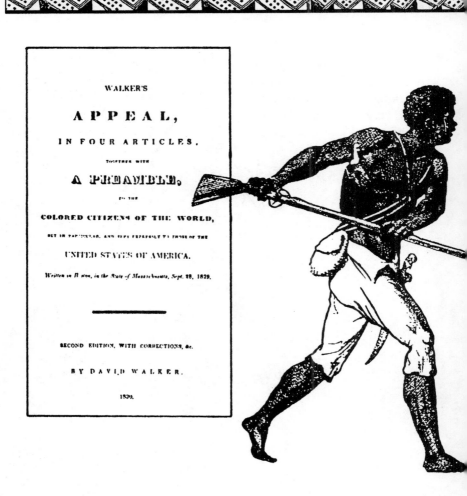

Many Blacks argued against these White chauvinist and Eurocentric Interpretations.

In 1829, **David Walker** (1785-1830) published his famous "Appeal," which condemned slavery and racism. He wrote that the glorious history of Africa (particularly Ancient Egypt) showed that Blacks were not inferior to any other race.

Henry Highland Garnet (1815-1882), an African-American abolitionist, echoed Walker's sentiments by praising the African heritage and urging its study.

Years later, in 1857, the African American **James Theodore Holly** (1828-1911) produced a booklet which connected the Haitian Revolution with African history and culture.

In searching their African past, Walker, Garnet and Holly found counter-arguments to the institution of slavery, the "backwardness" of America's African descendants, and Social Darwinism.

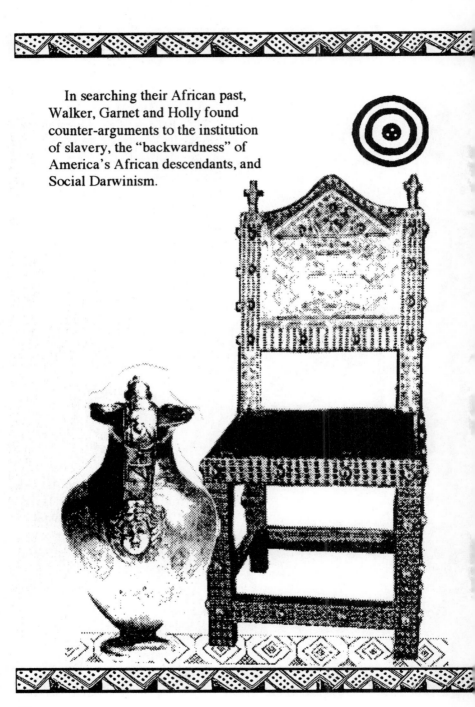

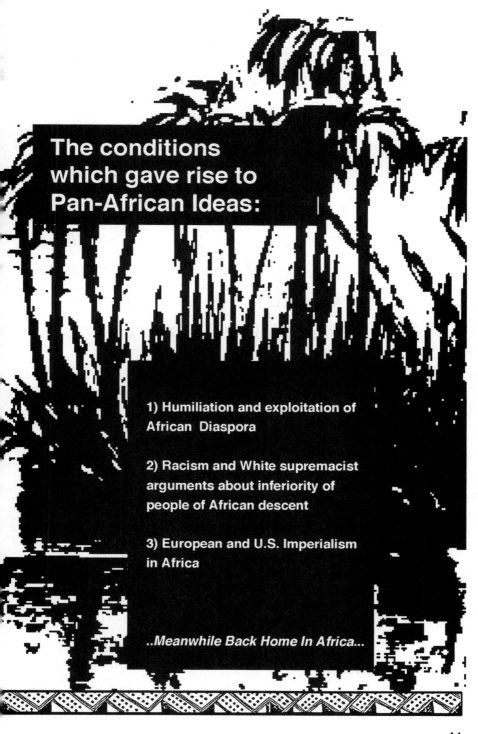

The conditions which gave rise to Pan-African Ideas:

1) Humiliation and exploitation of African Diaspora

2) Racism and White supremacist arguments about inferiority of people of African descent

3) European and U.S. Imperialism in Africa

..Meanwhile Back Home In Africa...

In the early 19th century, British IMPERIALISM was beginning to develop. But in order to grow it needed markets to dump cheap goods, and raw materials to feed its growing industries. The slave trade (triangular trade*) no longer was of benefit to the development of industrial capitalism. Realizing this, British imperialists outlawed the slave trade (1807) and slavery (1834).

* In the triangular trade, rum and trinkets from New England were traded for West African slaves and ivory, these were taken to the West Indes and traded for tobacco and molasses which were carried to New England.

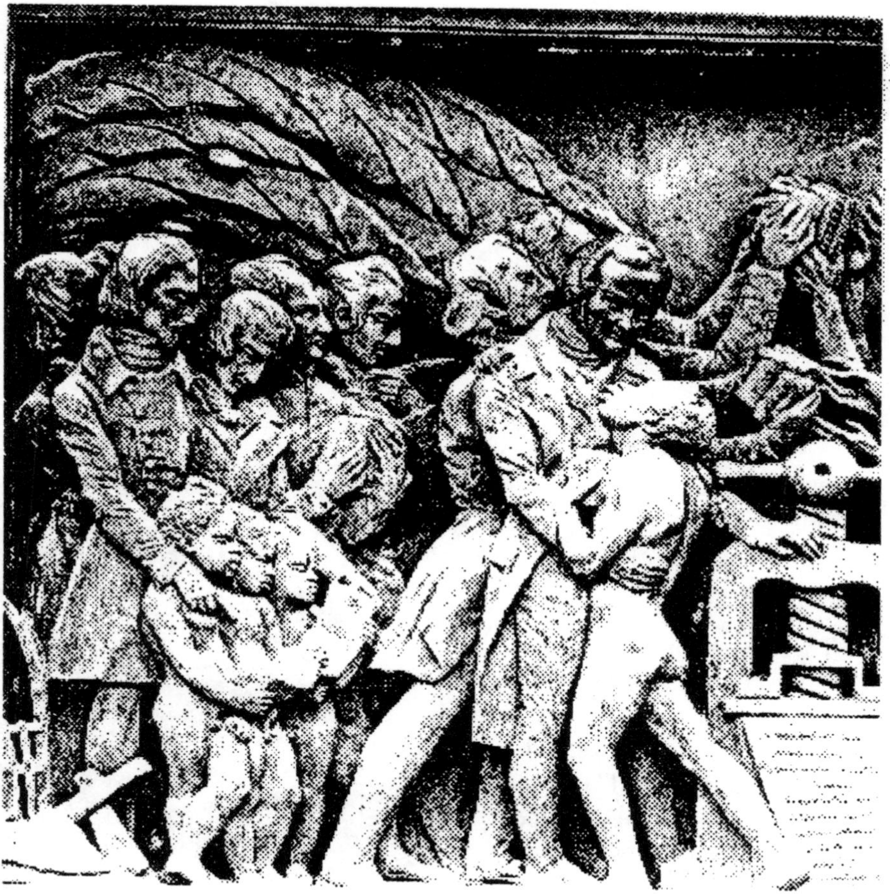

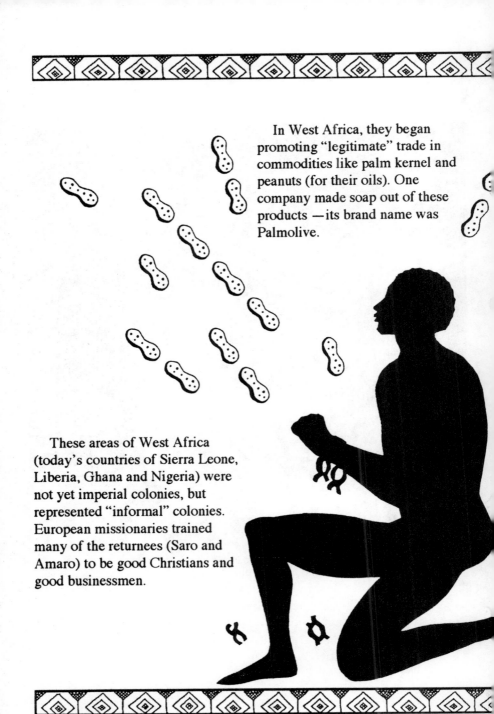

In West Africa, they began promoting "legitimate" trade in commodities like palm kernel and peanuts (for their oils). One company made soap out of these products —its brand name was Palmolive.

These areas of West Africa (today's countries of Sierra Leone, Liberia, Ghana and Nigeria) were not yet imperial colonies, but represented "informal" colonies. European missionaries trained many of the returnees (Saro and Amaro) to be good Christians and good businessmen.

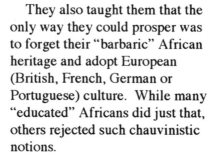They also taught them that the
only way they could prosper was
to forget their "barbaric" African
heritage and adopt European
(British, French, German or
Portuguese) culture. While many
"educated" Africans did just that,
others rejected such chauvinistic
notions.

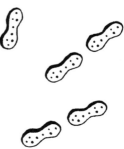

PAN-AFRICANISM AND AFRICAN NATIONALISM

Nations have not always existed.

Most evolved from stable, historically developed communities of people with a common territory, economy, culture, and language.

Such communities have existed for many years, but only in modern times have they become **nations**. Such nations (often dominated by outside powers) arose when a privileged class of the subject peoples rallied the rest of the people in an attempt to shake off foreign rule and establish its own state.

The economic and political base of such a movement has a class content. The privileged class, because of its position among the subject peoples (usually due to education or wealth), has the most to gain in such a movement. They become the new power once the old foreign power is dispatched. But in order to wage this struggle there must be an ideology to bond them together.

This is where nationalism comes in — it is a unifying belief that the interests of the nation-state (represented by the privileged class) and the people coincide — outweighing any other consideration.

From these notions developed modern nationalism:

a belief in and the practice of forming and maintaining a nation-state. Thus nations are social, political and economic, not "natural," formations.

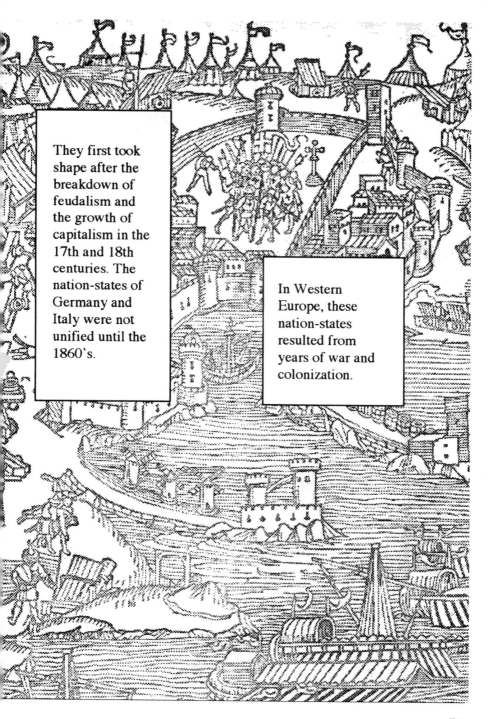

They first took shape after the breakdown of feudalism and the growth of capitalism in the 17th and 18th centuries. The nation-states of Germany and Italy were not unified until the 1860's.

In Western Europe, these nation-states resulted from years of war and colonization.

*Then in the late
19th century,
European
Imperialism began
carving out
colonies in Africa.*

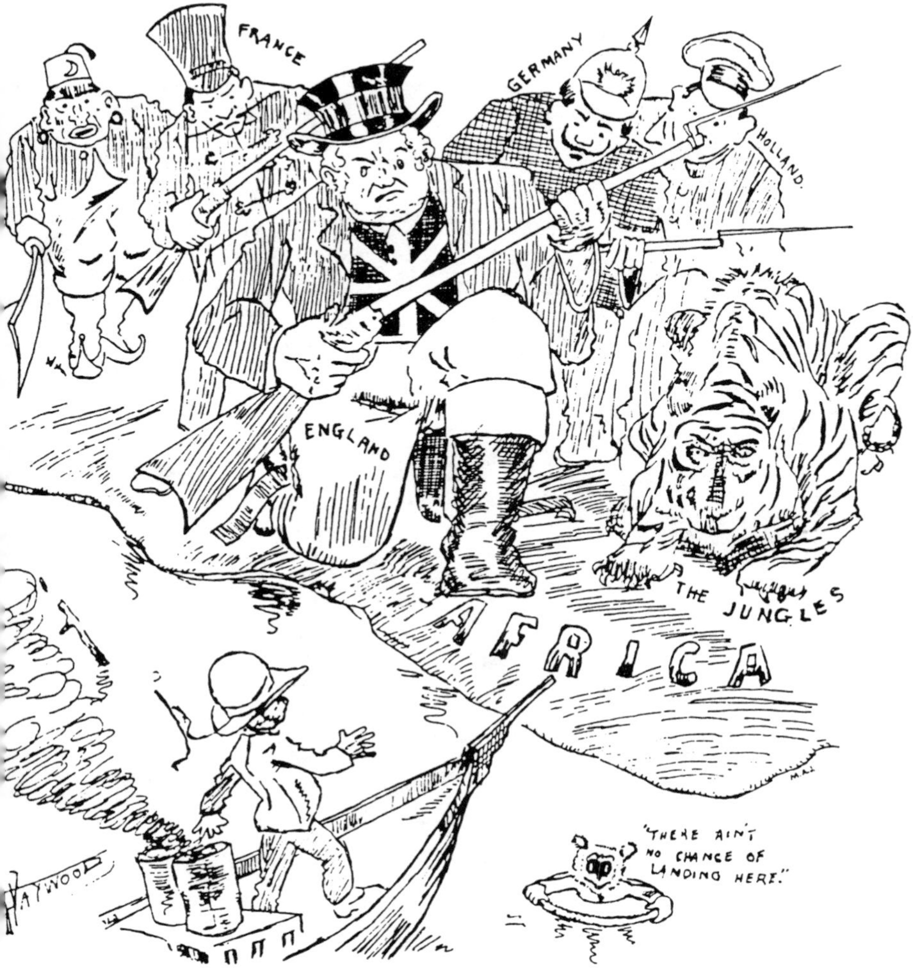
FRANCE
GERMANY
HOLLAND
ENGLAND
THE JUNGLES
AFRICA
"THERE AIN'T NO CHANCE OF LANDING HERE."
HAYWOOD

Soon after, African nationalism arose. Under the guidance of several very important pioneers, the idea of Pan-Africanism and African Nationalism

began to take shape in *West Africa.*

In their early stages the two movements intersected.

JAMES AFRICANUS BEALE HORTON:

was born in Sierra Leone in 1835. The British Anti-Slavery Squadron had rescued his mother from a slave ship and returned her to Freetown. Horton was educated in Sierra Leone and England where he took the name "Africanus" to show pride in his heritage. He became a medical doctor, and served in the British Army Medical Service for over 30 years. He also studied his own history. Horton wrote about the great African past and the possibility of an equally great future among "educated" (i.e. Europeanized) West African peoples. His Ideas contributed much to the spread of Pan-Africanism and African Nationalism in West Africa.

JAMES "HOLY" JOHNSON:

Like his classmate J.A.B. Horton, Johnson was also a Sierra Leonean from Igboland (Nigeria). He became an Anglican priest with the Church Missionary Society (C.M.S). Indeed, he spread Christianity with such zeal that he earned the nickname "Holy."

Johnson also believed in the future development of Africa, but only under the guidance of western (although Africanized) Christianity. Johnson preached that Africans all over the world had a unique character (which was later called the "African Personality").

EDWARD BLYDEN:

was probably the greatest promoter of Pan-Africanism of his time. Although later becoming a Liberian citizen, Blyden was born in the West Indies in 1832. His grandfather had been taken as a slave from his home in Nigeria. In 1851 Blyden left St. Thomas (then a Danish West Indian colony) and after some time in New York emigrated to Liberia.

He became editor of several newspapers, a Presbyterian minister, a professor (and later president) of Liberia College, a diplomat and full time promoter of Pan-Africanism. He wrote many brilliant books attacking racism. Like "Holy" Johnson, Blyden was also a devout Christian and wanted independent African churches.

57

Among them was a deep respect for Western education and institutions (including capitalism and Christianity),

pride in Africa's past.

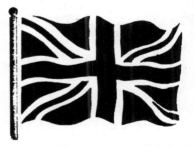

and a mistrust of British imperialism.

These commonalities led them to the belief that the only realistic solution to encroaching British imperialism and chauvinism was the creation of

African Nation-States

with complete autonomy in all affairs.

Ironically, Horton and Johnson worked to build Confederations or Western-style states (the Fanti Confederation and the Egba United Board of Management, respectively) that would promote English education, a parliamentary system and commerce for the benefit of Anglicized African merchants.

Thus at the end of the 19th century we have the first stirrings of African Nationalism. As Horton, Blyden and Johnson show, it was to be found almost exclusively among European educated Africans and Diasporans. They believed that they were the most qualified spokespersons for "their people." They called for national autonomy, the building of African nation-states and economic development.

African nationalism and Pan-Africanism had their proponents in the Diaspora as well.

TIMOTHY THOMAS FORTUNE (1856-1928), an African-American publisher, built upon the ideas of Johnson and other African Pan-Africanists. Ironically, he foresaw that European partition of Africa would eventually bring forth national entities and an organization of African unity. In 1890 Fortune helped found the **AFRO-AMERICAN LEAGUE,** which attempted to establish a national organization to promote these ideas in the U.S.

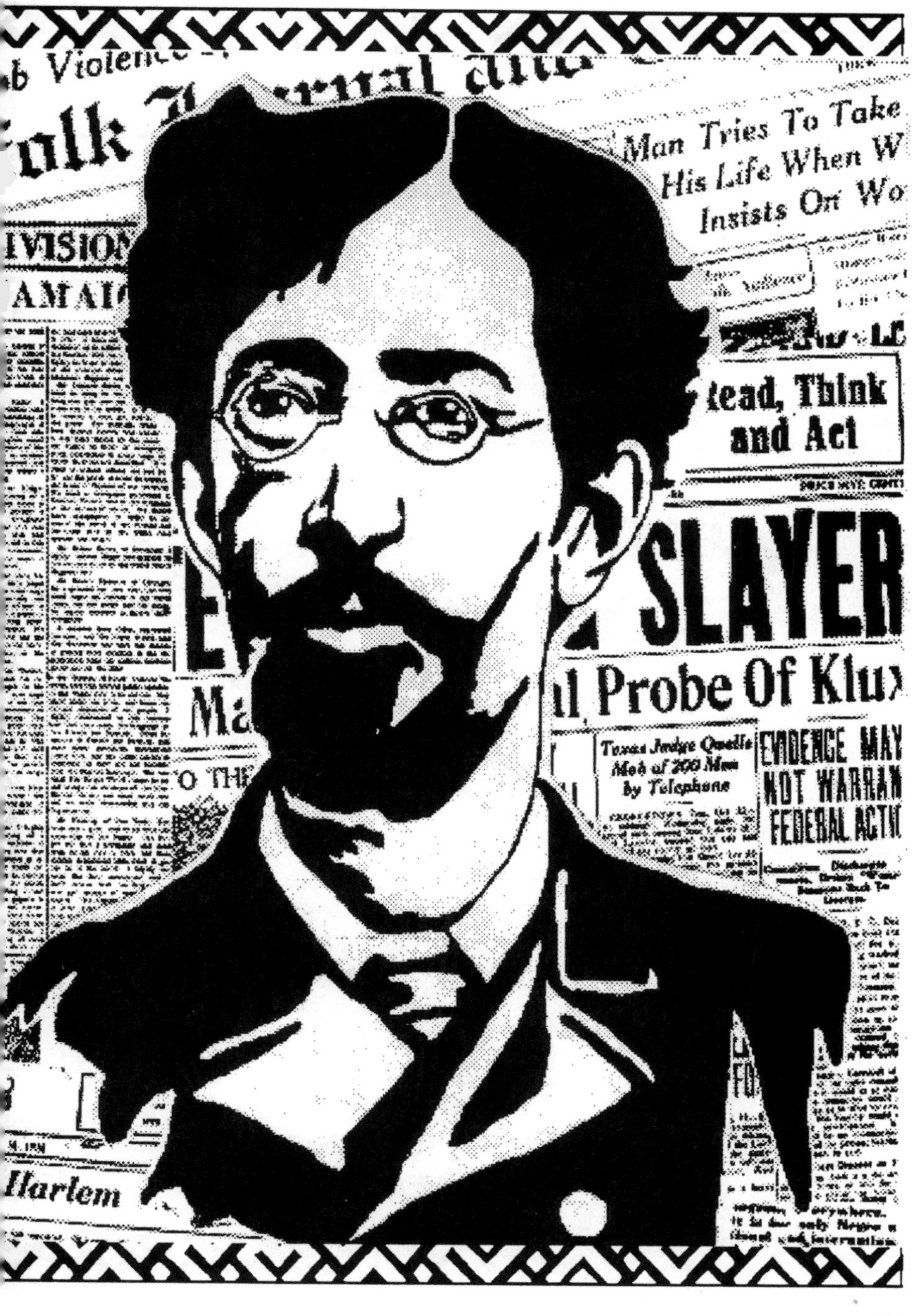
Man Tries To Take
His Life When W
Insists On Wo
ead, Think
and Act
SLAYER
l Probe Of Klu
Texas Judge Quells
Mob of 200 Men
by Telephone
EVIDENCE MAY
NOT WARRAN
FEDERAL ACTI
Harlem

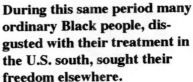

During this same period many ordinary Black people, disgusted with their treatment in the U.S. south, sought their freedom elsewhere.

In 1886, **GEORGE CHARLES**, president of The AFRICAN EMIGRATION ASSOCIATION, presented a petition to the U.S. Congress declaring that his organization planned to set up a United States of Africa.

BISHOP HENRY McNEIL TURNER (1833-1915), the leading advocate of the Back to Africa Movement at the time, became the inspiration for many. At his urging, thousands of Black people made plans "to seek the promised land." One such group of Black emigres, after first leaving Florida for Oklahoma territory, eventually headed for Savannah and boarded a ship home to Africa. Many others did the same, often going to Liberia or other West African destinations.

BENITO SYLVAIN:,

another diasporan nationalist, was
born in Haiti around 1868. He
studied in Haiti and France before
becoming a professional journalist.
He wrote many articles glorifying the
Haitian Revolution and the Black
slaves who 'kicked out Napoleon.'
Sylvain believed that Africans would
one day achieve nationhood and
arrive at their "hour of Glory."
Sylvain later acted as aide-de-camp to
Emperor Menelik of Abyssinia.

Pan-*Africanism*:

The Cultural Idea and the Political Movement.

In 1884, German Chancellor Otto von Bismarck called other European nations to a conference in Berlin. No Africans were invited. The 14 European countries (including the United States) sat at a table and carved up Africa as if it were a Christmas turkey. England got the biggest pieces; followed by France, Germany and Portugal. Even the Belgian king, Leopold II, was given the Congo and its people to rule and exploit. After this paper division, the European nations began the so-called "scramble for Africa." They took African land, natural resources, and forced the people to work for the European "mother country."

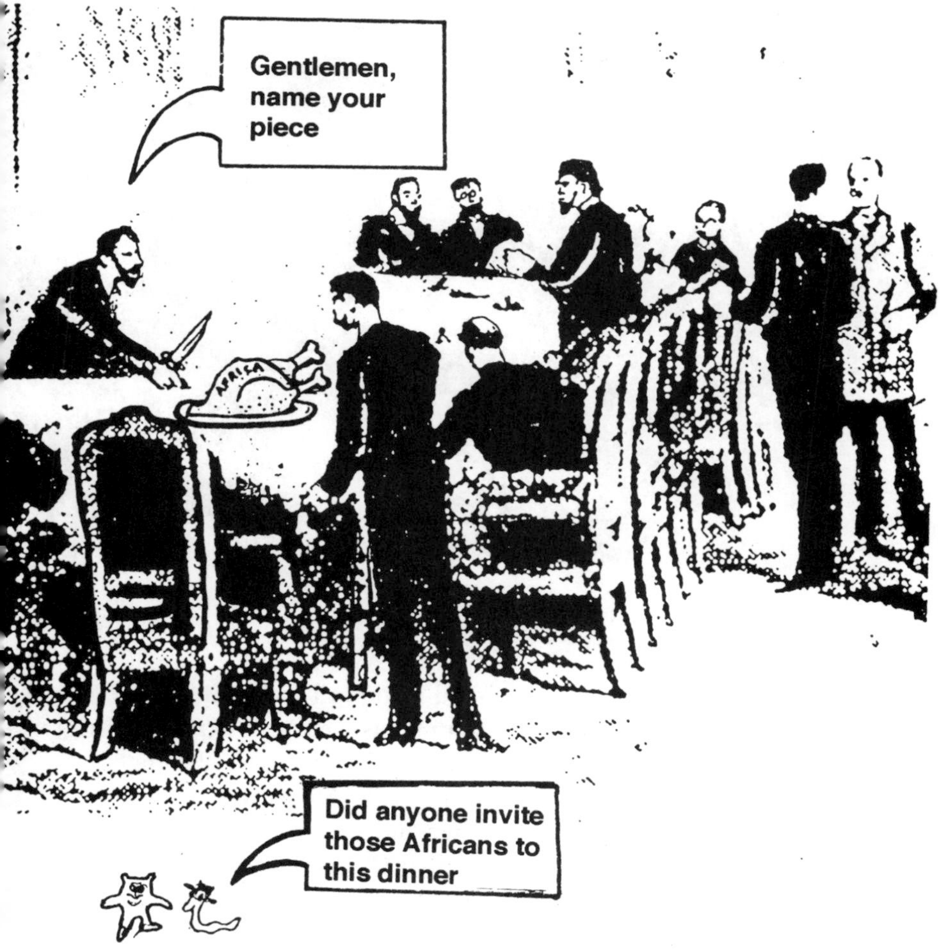
Gentlemen, name your piece
AFRICA
Did anyone invite those Africans to this dinner

Anti-European and Pan-African
sentiments were also expressed in
Atlanta, Georgia, two years later.
In 1895, the Steward Missionary
Foundation for Africa sponsored
another **CONGRESS ON AF-
RICA.** As with the Chicago
meeting, delegates discussed the
continuing Imperial threat.

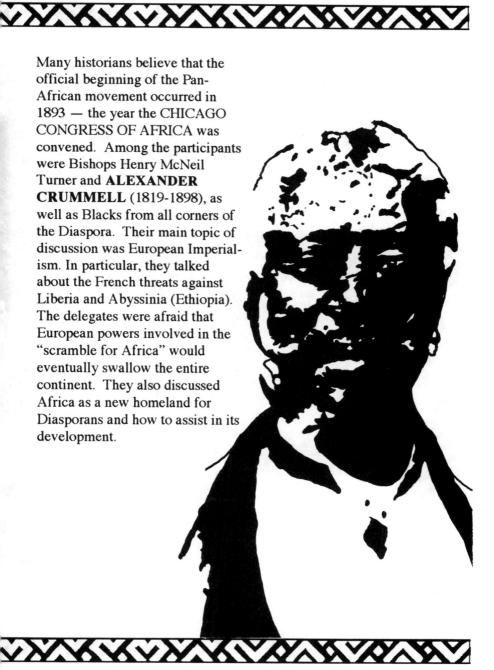

Many historians believe that the official beginning of the Pan-African movement occurred in 1893 — the year the CHICAGO CONGRESS OF AFRICA was convened. Among the participants were Bishops Henry McNeil Turner and **ALEXANDER CRUMMELL** (1819-1898), as well as Blacks from all corners of the Diaspora. Their main topic of discussion was European Imperialism. In particular, they talked about the French threats against Liberia and Abyssinia (Ethiopia). The delegates were afraid that European powers involved in the "scramble for Africa" would eventually swallow the entire continent. They also discussed Africa as a new homeland for Diasporans and how to assist in its development.

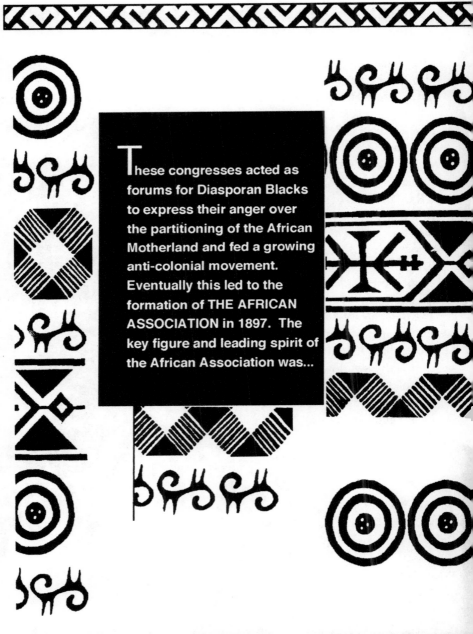

These congresses acted as forums for Diasporan Blacks to express their anger over the partitioning of the African Motherland and fed a growing anti-colonial movement. Eventually this led to the formation of THE AFRICAN ASSOCIATION in 1897. The key figure and leading spirit of the African Association was...

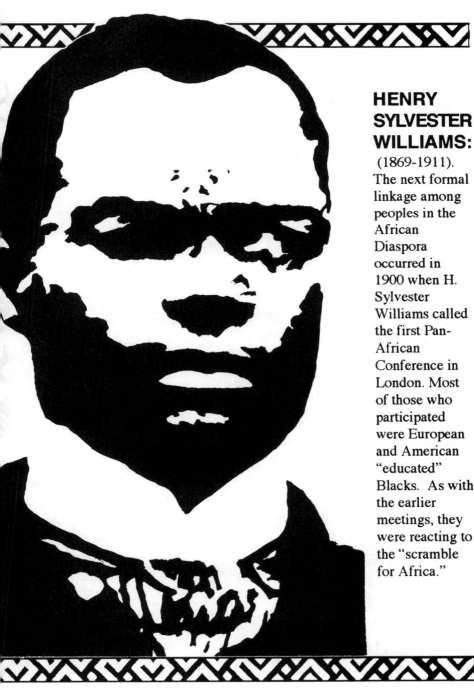

HENRY SYLVESTER WILLIAMS:

(1869-1911). The next formal linkage among peoples in the African Diaspora occurred in 1900 when H. Sylvester Williams called the first Pan-African Conference in London. Most of those who participated were European and American "educated" Blacks. As with the earlier meetings, they were reacting to the "scramble for Africa."

Thirty delegates attended the conference including H.S. Williams and his chief aide, **BISHOP ALEXANDER WALTERS (1858-1917).** Also at this meeting was a young man who later became the main figure of the movement,

Aside from discussing the bad treatment of African peoples, the conference participants talked about bringing people of African descent into closer communication

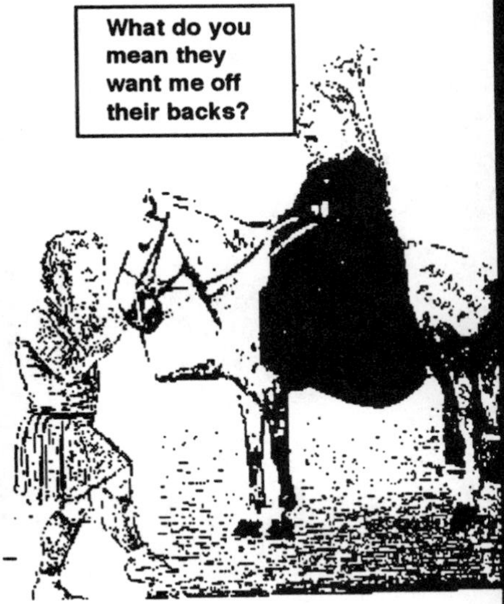
What do you mean they want me off their backs?
AFRICAN PEOPLE

with one another. They proposed starting a movement which would demand full rights for African people. After the conference, the delegates sent a petition to Queen Victoria protesting the treatment of Africans, particularly those in Southern Africa.

HENRY SYLVESTER WILLIAMS:
Was born in Trinidad in 1869. He later studied Law in London and made contact with African students there. In 1897 Williams founded the AFRICAN ASSOCIATION, and in 1900 became secretary of the PAN-AFRICAN ASSOCIATION (PAA) — an organization which grew out of the First Pan-African Conference.

In 1903 Williams went to South Africa to practice Law. While there he and **FRANCIS PEREGRINO (1851-1919),** a Ghana-born journalist and PAA representative, advised the African Kings Lerotholi and Lewanika.

Peregrino stayed in South Africa until his death. Williams left in 1904, after receiving death threats. He returned to London, where he continued to work with PAA until he died in 1911. While many consider Du Bois the "Father of Pan- Africanism," H.S. Williams can be seen as the **"Grandfather."**

THE PEDRO GORINO

The Adventures of a Negro Sea-Captain
in Africa and on the Seven Seas in his
attempts to Found an Ethiopian Empire

An Autobiographical Narrative

By

CAPTAIN HARRY DEAN

WRITTEN WITH THE ASSISTANCE OF
STERLING NORTH

also HARRY DEAN, a black American sea captain and descendant of Paul Cuffe, advised King Sigcawu Mqikela of Mpondo.

Two Pan-

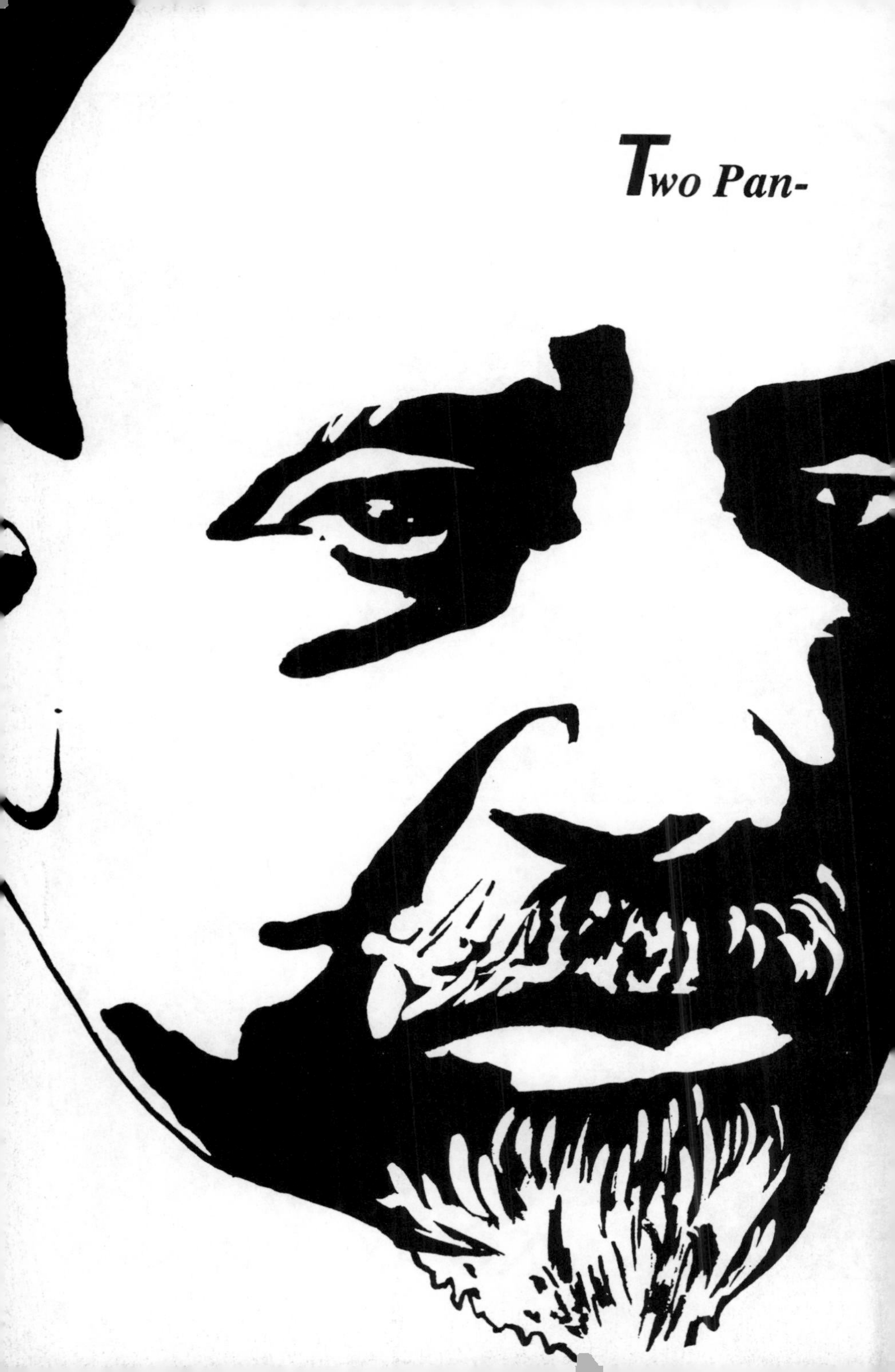

African Giants

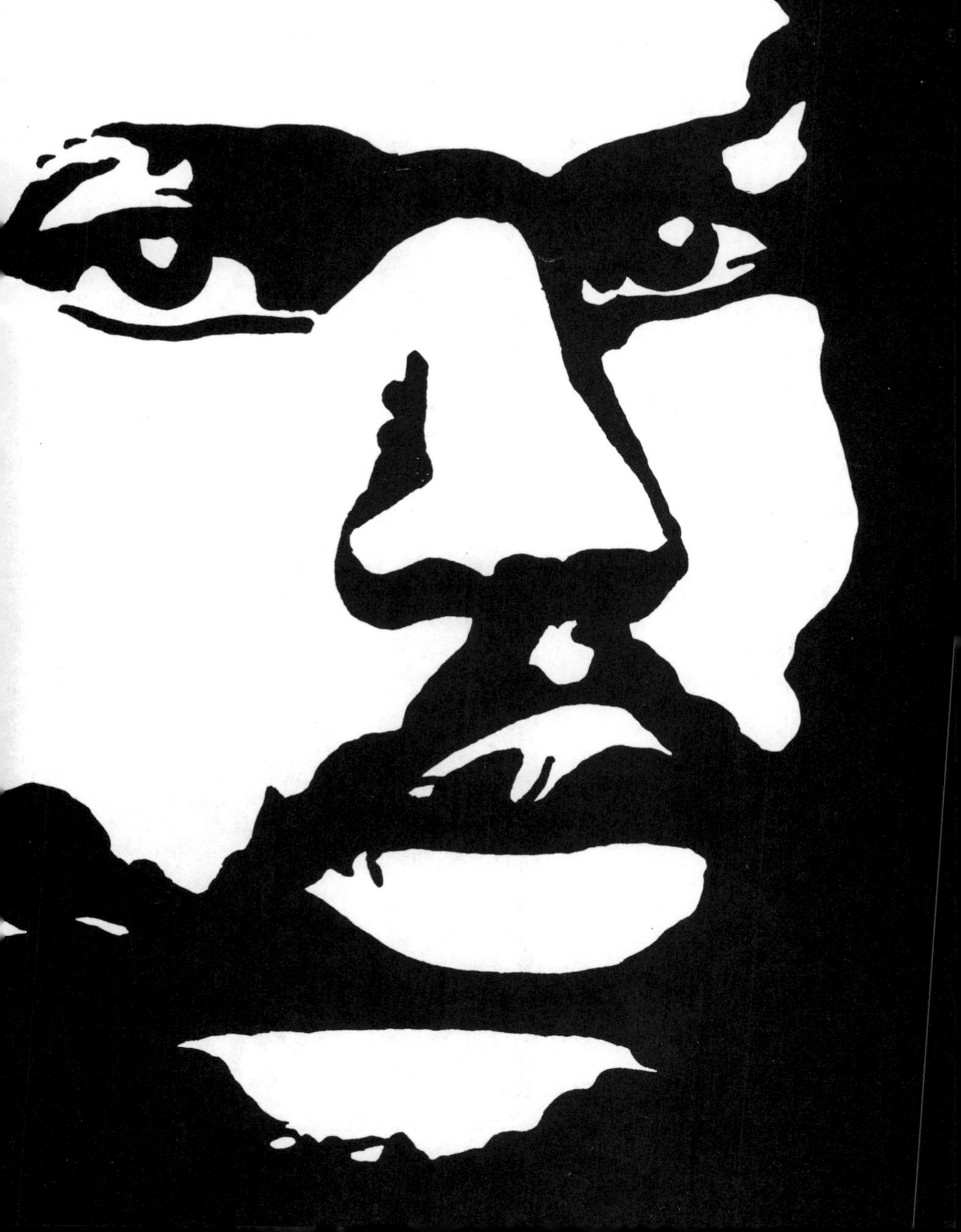

Although there were many important individuals in the early stages of Pan-Africanism, the two most prominent figures were W.E.B. Du Bois and MARCUS GARVEY (1887-1940). Over the years, Du Bois and Garvey developed a heated rivalry.

They were opposites in both personality and method of spreading Pan- African thought; yet each worked towards the same end. Both sought to restore dignity and self-determination to Black people throughout the world.

W.E.B. DU BOIS

was born in Great Barrington, Massachusetts on February 23, 1868. A Ph.d. graduate of Harvard University, he authored over twenty books on Black history and culture.

Early in his career Du Bois worked with White American liberals in the **NIAGARA MOVEMENT and the NATIONAL ASSOCIATION FOR THE ADVANCEMENT OF COLORED PEOPLE (NAACP)**.

But after the first Pan-African Congress he changed his attitude. The deteriorating conditions for Blacks convinced him that Black people had to fight for their own advancement. Yet, unlike Garvey, Du Bois did not preach separatism. Instead, he saw the problems of Diasporan Black and Africans as part of an international struggle of oppressed people for freedom and Justice.

Garvey, on the other hand, saw the problem in cultural, economic and psychological terms. He believed the basic problem was that Blacks lacked knowledge and pride in their African ancestry and ... therefore could not counter white racism.

The ultimate solution was returning to Africa and building their own state. Along with his first wife,

AMY ASHWOOD GARVEY, he formed the **Universal Negro Improvement Association (UNIA)** in 1914. The organization promoted the slogans "**back to Africa**" and "**Africa for the Africans.**"

Marcus Garvey and The Black Parliaments

In 1916, Garvey's UNIA moved from Jamaica to Harlem, New York. Soon Marcus called for a large international convention, known as **THE FIRST BLACK PARLIAMENT.** At the first meeting Garvey adopted guidelines which formed the basis for all succeeding Pan-African organizations.

Garvey based The Black Parliaments and the UNIA on mass appeal for symbols and ceremonies: He encouraged Blacks to recognize their glorious African past. He conferred titles like "Duke of the Nile" and "Earl of the Congo" on his followers. However, while Garvey and his followers worked to return to Africa, there was little stress on the political or economic realities of Imperialism. Nonetheless, Garvey tried to instill a sense of self-dignity in Black people, who had been ravaged by slavery and colonialism.

In addition to Garvey's cultural uplift programs, there were important business ventures. They included:

1) BLACK STAR LINES
(an international commercial and passenger steamship line)

2) AFRICAN COMMERCIAL LEAGUE/AFRICAN FACTORIES CORPORATION (ran small businesses in Harlem)

3) LIBERIAN CONSTRUCTION LOAN (a fund-raising scheme to develop Liberia and over take it)

4) LIBERTY UNIVERSITY
(a vocational training school in Virginia modeled after Washington's Tuskegee Institute)

GARVEYISM IN AFRICA

In the twenties, Garveyism was the most popular form of Pan-Africanism among West Indians and African-Americans. But it also interested some Africans, many of whom added their own interpretations.

In South Africa, the interest in Garveyism was connected to the spiritual philosophy of millenarianism and nationalist politics.

In West Africa, most who joined the movement were European educated elites interested more in the UNIA business programs (especially the Black Star Line) and commercial gain than the political or spiritual aspects.

One of the first Africans to show an early interest in Garveyism was **E. CASELY HAYFORD** (1866-1930). Hayford, a Fante (Ghanaian) lawyer, journalist, politician, and Pan-African theorist, was editor of the Gold Coast Leader, an influential Nationalist and Pan-Africanist newspaper.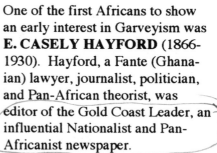
He was a founding member of the **ABORIGINES' RIGHTS PROTECTION SOCIETY and (with HERBERT MACUALAY, 1864-1946) NATIONAL CONGRESS OF BRITISH WEST AFRICA.** Casely Hayford spoke favorably of the **UNIA,** especially its business aspects. Ironically, his book *Ethiopia Unbound* (1911), had an great influence on Garvey's thought. In the early 1920's Casely Hayford was "knighted" by Garvey for his contributions to Pan-Africanism.

Another African who influenced Garvey was **DUSE MOHAMMED ALI** (1867-1944), an Egyptian of Sudanese ancestry. Duse was active in Pan-African circles in London where he tutored the young Garvey. Duse, with help from Casely Hayford and others, edited the influential **AFRICAN TIMES AND ORIENT REVIEW** — an early attempt to combine Pan-Africanism, Pan-Arabism and "Orientalism"

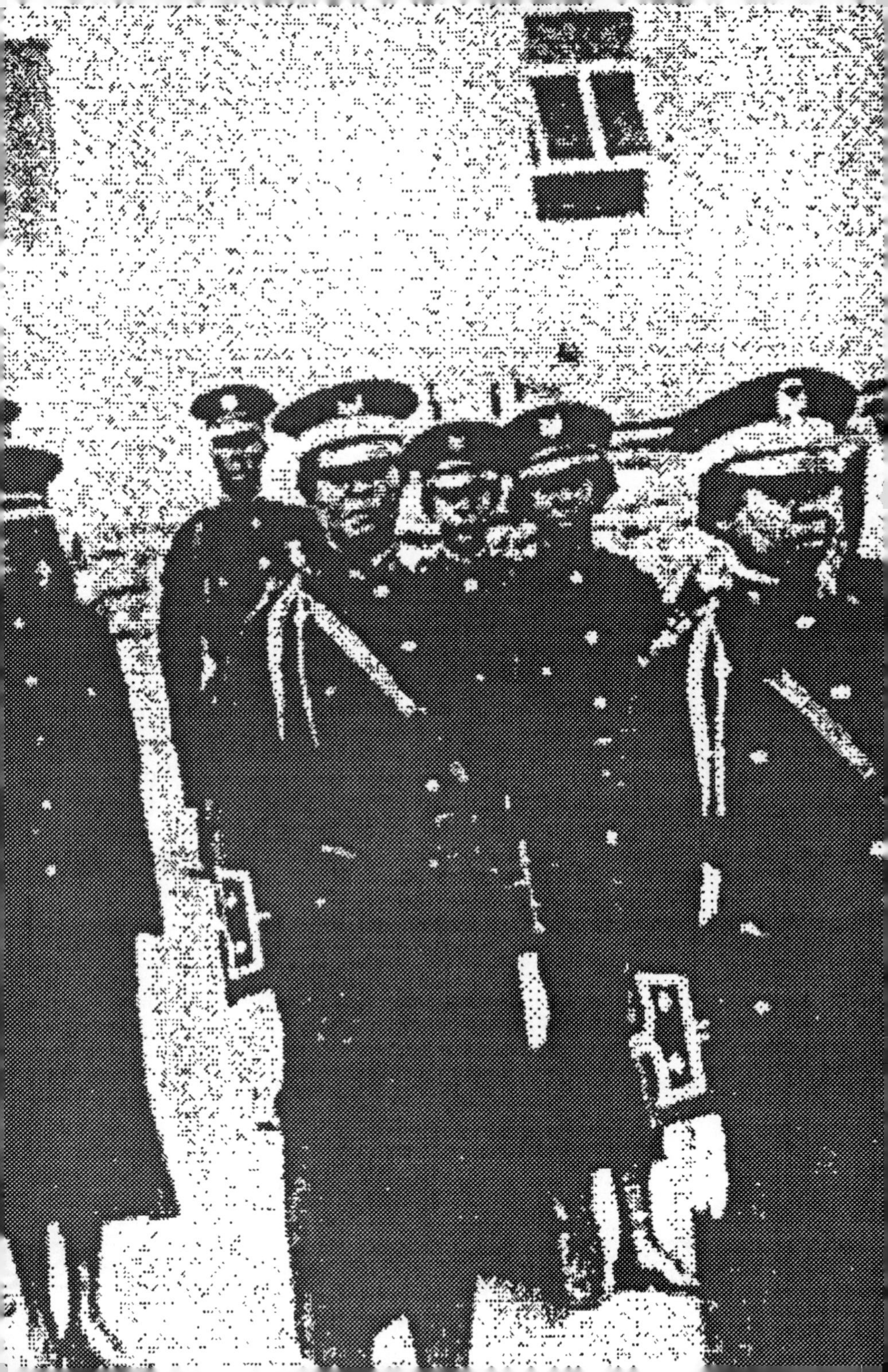

*W*omen in the Garvey Movement

Women were active in the Garvey Movement from the start. **AMY ASHWOOD** (Garvey's first wife) cofounded the movement in Jamaica. After leaving the **UNIA** she travelled and wrote on West Africa, England and Jamaica. She became involved in Jamaican politics and, in London, with a left coalition protesting the Italian invasion of Ethiopia.(1934) Eventually, she opened a restaurant in London that served as a meeting place for West African student activists (and future Pan-Africanists) like Kwame Nkrumah (1909-72) and Jomo Kenyatta (1891-1978).

Garvey's second wife, **AMY JACQUES,** was also very active. Indeed, from 1925-27 she actually ran the organization when Marcus was in jail. While men dominated the UNIA (and the Pan-African movement in general), women like **HENRIETTA VINTON DAVIS** (director of Black Star Lines) and Mme. **M.T.L. DE MENA** had long careers as **UNIA** officers and organizers. Others, like **QUEEN MOTHER MOORE, LAURA KOFEY** and **MITTIE MAUD LENA GORDON** were not only **UNIA** organizers, but also involved in other Pan-Africanist issues.

Queen Mother Moore (1898-1978?) was active in the Harlem branch of the UNIA. She worked with leftist organizations including the Communist Party (USA) and the Italo-Ethiopia Committee in the 1930's.

Laura Kofey, who claimed to be of African birth, organized for the UNIA in Florida. Later, after becoming disillusioned with Garvey, Kofey began her own colonization movement rivaling the UNIA. She died under very mysterious circumstances, not long after leaving the UNIA.

Mittie Maud Lena Gordon organized for the UNIA in the Chicago area; but like Laura Kofey, later began her own rival repatriation movement. Gordon also worked closely with the white racist Senator Theodore Bilbo of Mississippi (as did Amy Jacques Garvey), both sharing the desire to see Blacks leave the United States for Africa.

Each of these women was a
prime mover in the movement.
Aside from the women in
leadership (each chapter had a
"lady president"), women also
controlled the Black Cross
Nurses and made up most of
the mass membership in many
regions. Yet they faced
resistance (and often outright
hostility) from the male
dominated officers and
membership.

One of the most active women
members in fighting such male
chauvinism was the Feminist/
Pan-Africanist, ADELAIDE
CASELY HAYFORD.

ADELAIDE CASELY HAYFORD:

was born Adelaide Smith in 1868. She came from an elite "Creole" (Saro) family in colonial Freetown, Sierra Leone. At an early age her family moved to England. Adelaide was educated in England and Germany, and later met and married Joseph E. Casely Hayford, the distinguished Pan-Africanist. She served briefly as the "lady president" of the Freetown branch of the UNIA. In the 1920's she founded, with KATHLEEN EASMON, a school for African girls in Freetown. She also participated in the 1927 Pan-African Congress in New York. As an African and a feminist, she added scope to Garvey's style of Pan-Africanism. Her daughter, GLADYS CASELY HAYFORD, was a Harlem Renaissance poetess.

"The problem of the twentieth century is the problem of the colour line — the relation of the darker to the lighter races of men in Asia and Africa, in America and the islands of the sea."

W.E.B. Du Bois

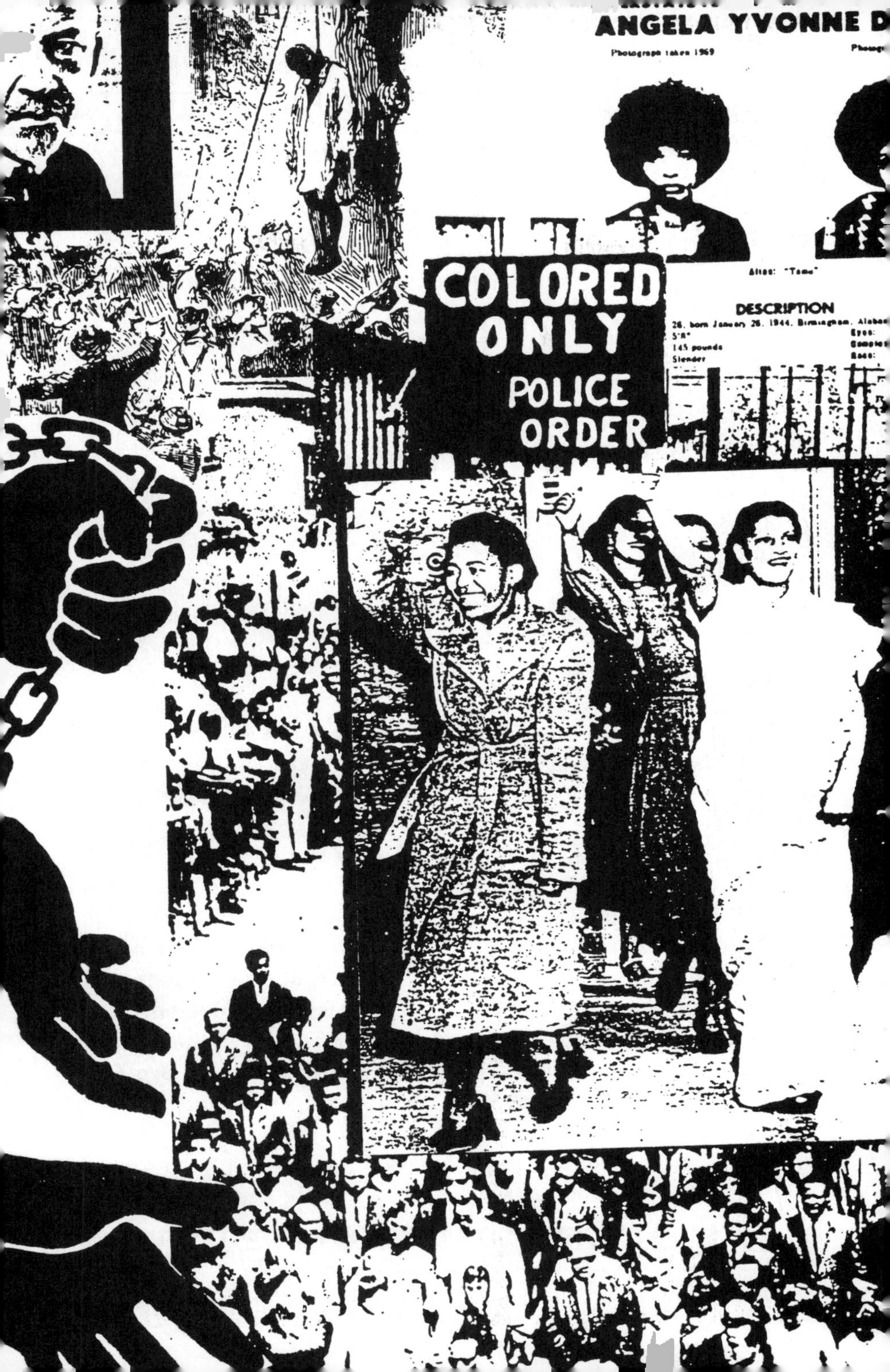
ANGELA YVONNE D
Photograph taken 1969
Alias: "Tamu"
DESCRIPTION
26, born January 26, 1944, Birmingham, Alaba
145 pounds
Slender
COLORED
ONLY
POLICE
ORDER

The First Du Bois Pan-African Congress

While Garvey was promoting Pan-Africanist ideas with his organization, W.E.B. Du Bois set about creating a forum for his concepts. He tried to rekindle Pan-African interest through a series of Pan-African Congresses (modeled after H. Sylvester Williams' Conference of 1900.) The first of these meetings was held in Paris in 1919 to coincide with the Paris Peace Conference at the end of the First Imperialist World War.

Du Bois believed he could convince the Imperialist powers that President Woodrow Wilson's principle of self-determination should apply to Africa. Somewhat naively, he hoped they would see that Africans could rule themselves. The delegates to the Pan-African Congress adopted a long resolution that declared the need for international laws to protect Africans.

The Second Du Bois Pan-African Congress

Three additional Du Bois Pan-African Congresses took place before the Second Imperialist World War. The Second Pan-African Congress was held in London and Brussels in 1921. Many considered it as the most radical of the Congresses. Most of the speakers openly criticized colonial policy as well as the poor quality of life in the Americas. The resolutions passed at the end of the sessions were critical of European and American imperialism and racism. These resolutions became known as the Declaration to the World, or simply the **LONDON MANIFESTO.**

They also called for African land to be held in "trust." They insisted that the imperialist powers give Africans the right to participate in government "as quickly as their development permitted." But the resolution carefully avoided any mention of the African's right to independence. The idealism of the delegates, while noble, was unsuccessful in swaying the realities of global imperialism.

Several distinguished "ladies of the Negro race," attended the Second Pan-African Congress. The delegates included **JESSIE FAUSET (1884-1961), HELEN CURTIS and MRS. I.G. HUNT** (1862-1957)

JESSE FAUCET:

was literary editor of the Crisis, the organ of the **NAACP,** and an avid Pan-Africanist.

Helen Curtis, an African-American teacher, social worker, missionary, and **NAACP** and **YWCA/YMCA** activist, was the widow of the former U.S. consul general to Liberia. She travelled extensively in West Africa and Europe and headed the industrial department at Monrovia College, Liberia (1924-27).

Mrs. I.G. Hunt was also an active Pan-Africanist who, along with

ADDIE W. HUNTON:

(U.S.) and ANN MARIE (France) were on the international organizing committee for the 1921 Congress. Hunton, a major leader in the Black Women's Club movement, helped organize the Fourth Pan-African Congress in New York in 1927. All these women contributed significantly to the radical tone of the Second Pan-African Congress.

The Third and Fourth Du Bois Congresses

The Third (1923) and Fourth (1927) Pan-African Congresses changed only slightly in their position on the condemnation of racist policies. These were the last Congresses under the direct control of Du Bois — and the last for many years.

Garvey's Parliaments were much more popular than Du Bois' Congresses, yet in retrospect/ looking back both Pan-Africanist movements were idealistic and naive. The movement, under both Garvey and Du Bois, sought to Africanize exploitation, rather than to challenge directly European and American imperialism. They sought to replace the white/European exploiter class with one of African descent.

These political divisions continued during the Great Depression of the thirties. They were probably responsible for the lack of any Congressional confabs until after World War II. However, during the inter-war period cultural and political movements connected to Radical Black Nationalism, the Harlem Renaissance, Negritude and Ethiopianism, carried forth the message of Pan-Africanism — although not in a formalized movement.

In the period after the First Imperialist World War II a new mood of protest grew in the U.S., particularly in the Harlem section of New York.

WE DEMAND WORK OR WAGES

FIGHT — POLICE BRUTALITY

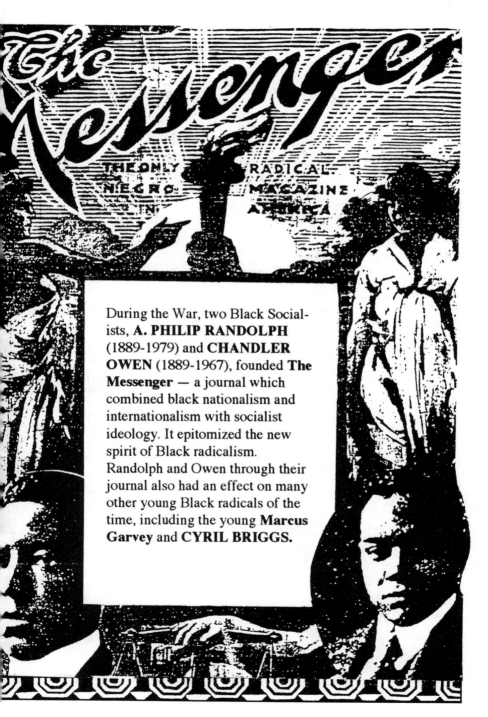

During the War, two Black Socialists, **A. PHILIP RANDOLPH** (1889-1979) and **CHANDLER OWEN** (1889-1967), founded **The Messenger** — a journal which combined black nationalism and internationalism with socialist ideology. It epitomized the new spirit of Black radicalism. Randolph and Owen through their journal also had an effect on many other young Black radicals of the time, including the young **Marcus Garvey** and **CYRIL BRIGGS.**

Briggs, who was born in the West Indies (Saint Kitts), was at one time an editor of the Black New York newspaper the **AMSTERDAM NEWS.** Between 1917-19 Briggs, along with other West Indian and African-American socialists, founded the underground revolutionary organization the **AFRICAN BLOOD BROTHERHOOD** (ABB). ABB was the first organization based in the U.S. which connected the struggle of Blacks in the Americas and Africa. Since iit was a secret organization, ABB leaders never recruited a mass membership, yet the organization's influence was great.

At its height in 1921, ABB claimed close to 3,000 members — spread over fifty posts in the U.S., the West Indies and Latin America. Its magazine, **THE CRUSADER,** claimed a circulation of 33,000. The ABB was briefly associated with the UNIA before being expelled in 1922. In the late 1920's many of the Blood Brotherhood's members (including Cyril Briggs) joined the Communist Party U.S.A. There they carried on the struggle for African liberation and African-American equal rights.

We are related —
you and I

You from the West
Indies,

I from Kentucky

We are related —
you and I

You from Africa

I from these States

We are brothers
— you and I.

Langston Hughes

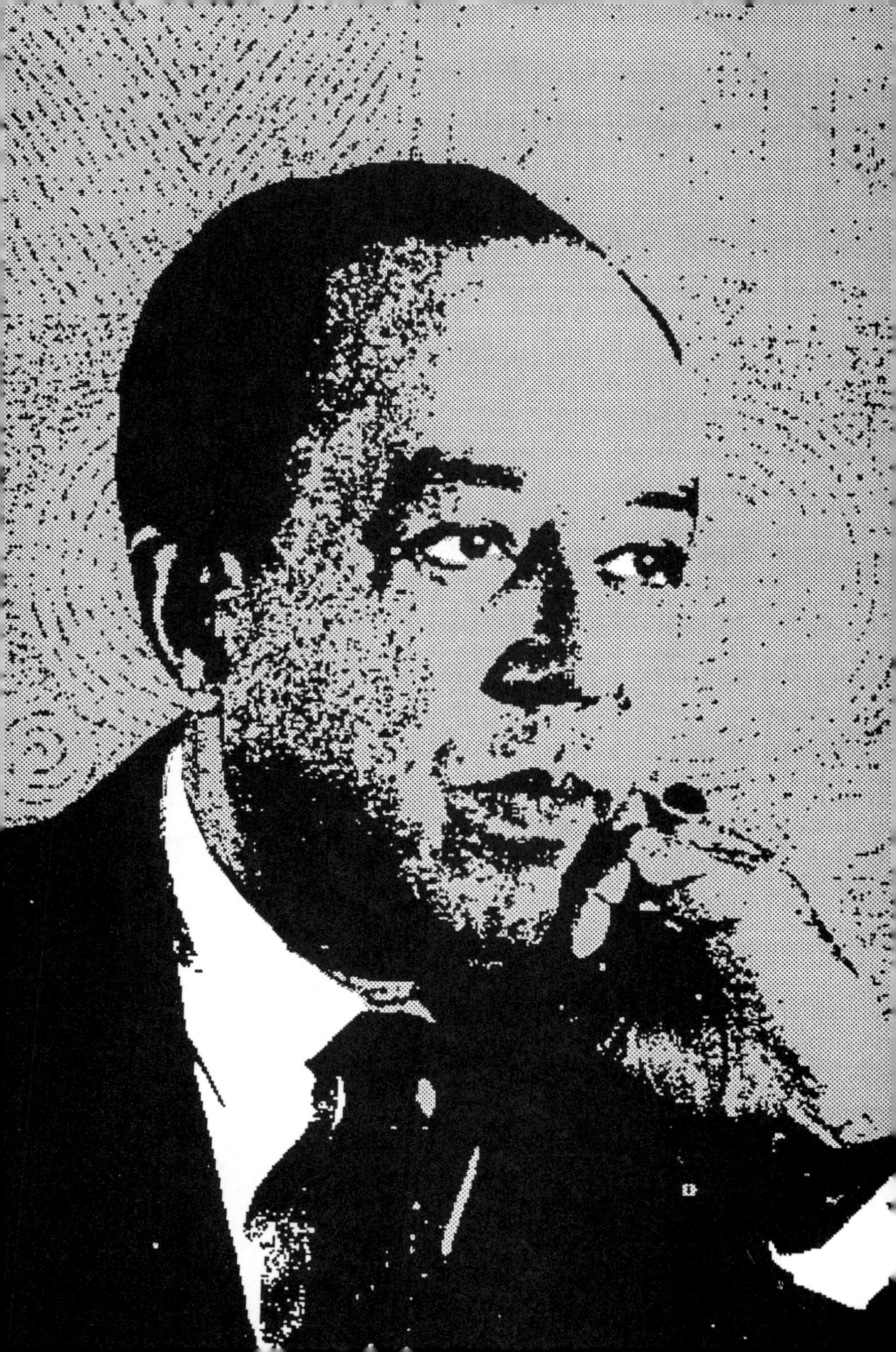

*T*HE HARLEM RENAISSANCE

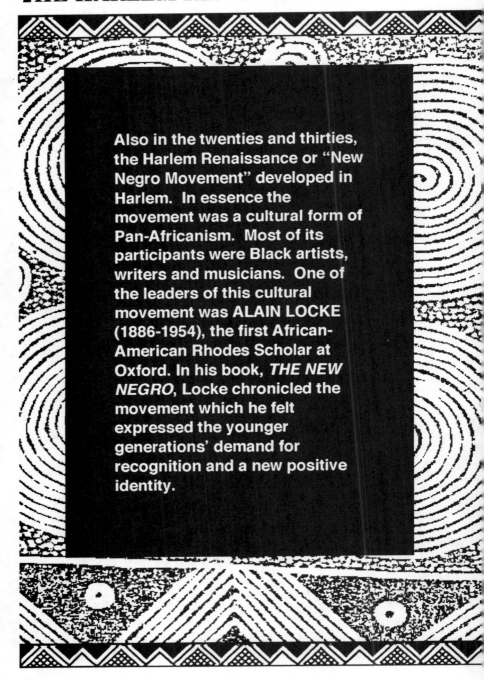

Also in the twenties and thirties, the Harlem Renaissance or "New Negro Movement" developed in Harlem. In essence the movement was a cultural form of Pan-Africanism. Most of its participants were Black artists, writers and musicians. One of the leaders of this cultural movement was ALAIN LOCKE (1886-1954), the first African-American Rhodes Scholar at Oxford. In his book, *THE NEW NEGRO*, Locke chronicled the movement which he felt expressed the younger generations' demand for recognition and a new positive identity.

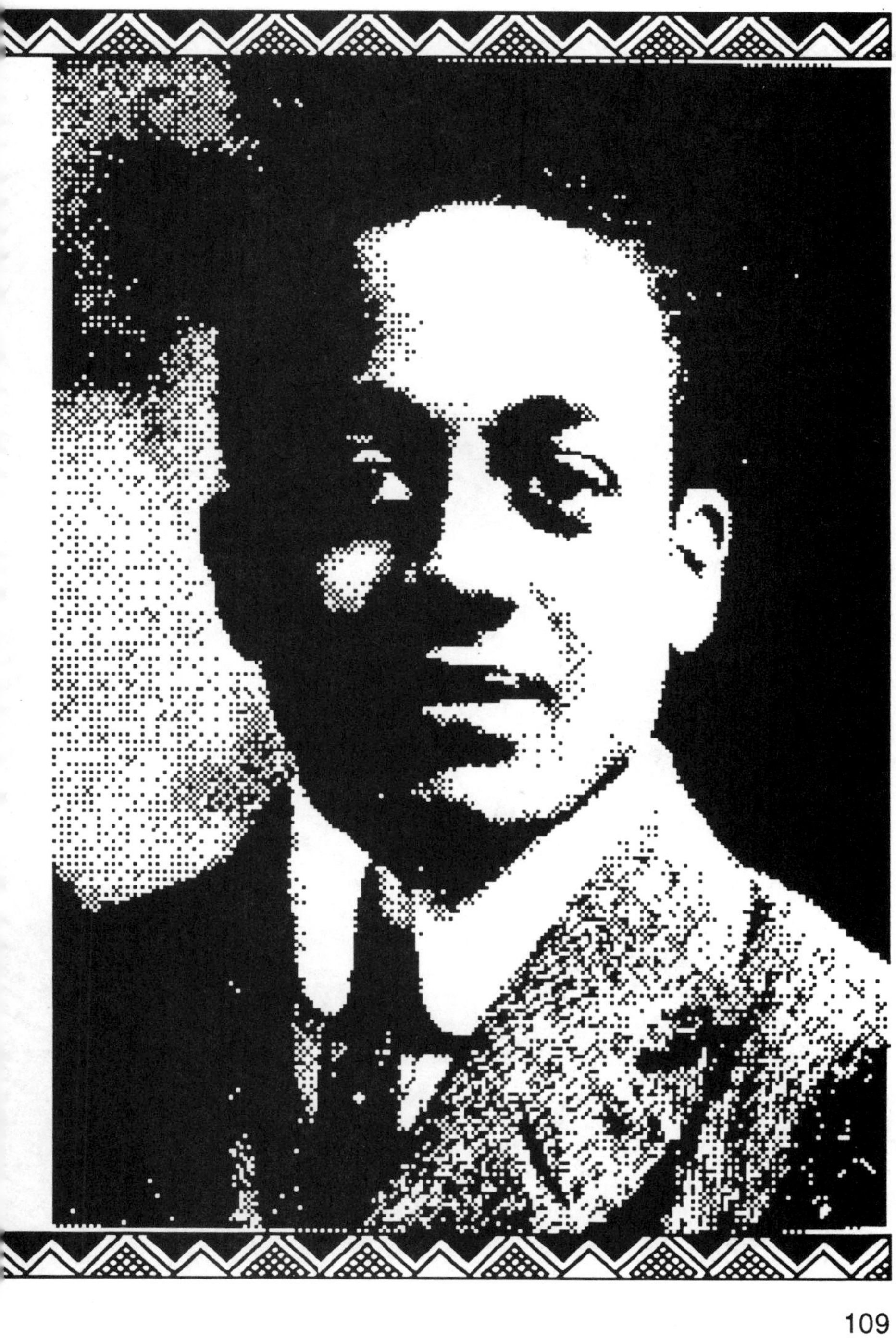

*W*riters

Among the many
writers who were a
part of the movement were

ZORA NEAL HURSTON

CLAUDE MCKAY

W.E.B. DUBO

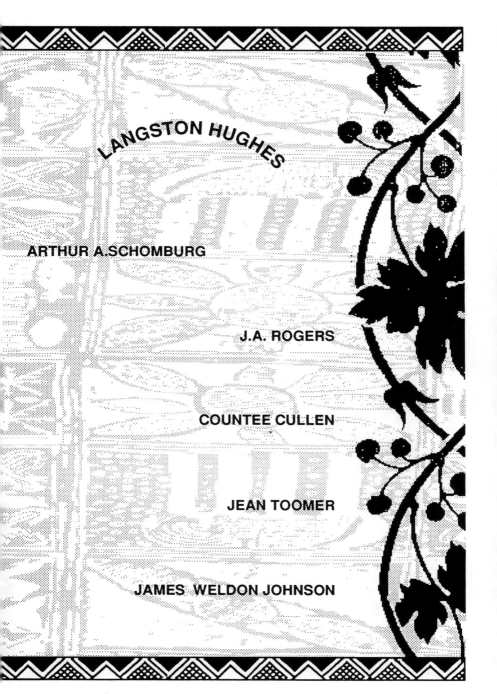

LANGSTON HUGHES

ARTHUR A. SCHOMBURG

J.A. ROGERS

COUNTEE CULLEN

JEAN TOOMER

JAMES WELDON JOHNSON

Actors, musicians and composers

Theatre and music were other important outlets for Black artists during the Harlem Renaissance. Actors, musicians, and composers like

PAUL ROBESON

CHARLES GILPIN

ETHEL WATERS

PAUL GREEN

GEORGE WALKER

BERT WILLIAMS

EUBIE BLAKE

NOBLE SISSLE

J. ROSAMOND JOHNSON

W.C. HANDY

DUKE ELLINGTON, KATHARINE DUNHAM and JOSEPHINE BAKER became legends all over the world.

113

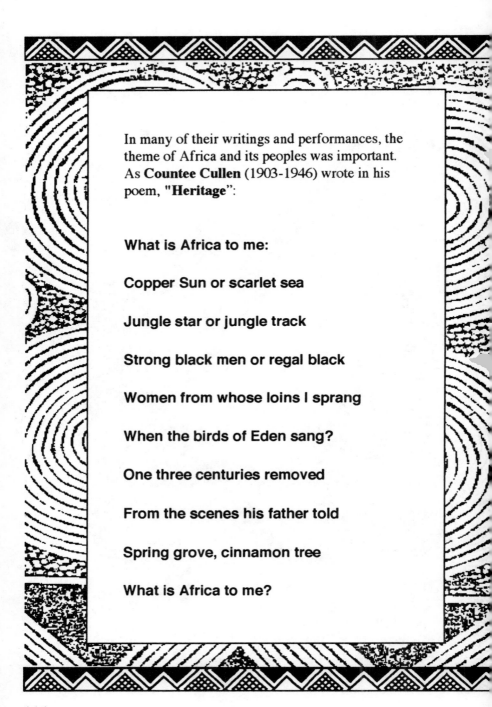

In many of their writings and performances, the theme of Africa and its peoples was important. As **Countee Cullen** (1903-1946) wrote in his poem, **"Heritage"**:

What is Africa to me:

Copper Sun or scarlet sea

Jungle star or jungle track

Strong black men or regal black

Women from whose loins I sprang

When the birds of Eden sang?

One three centuries removed

From the scenes his father told

Spring grove, cinnamon tree

What is Africa to me?

The pride which Harlem Renaissance writers and artists felt in their African ancestry, despite attempts by many whites to degrade and deny its importance, was woven into their sense of self. This pride enabled them to confirm their heritage and culture, which they conveyed to other African-Americans through literature, music and drama.

CLAUDE MCKAY:

was considered the Harlem Renaissance's first important author. Born in Jamaica (1889), he came to the U.S. in 1912. After studying at Tuskeegee Institute, he headed for New York where the Harlem Renaissance was just beginning to blossom. He published poems, short stories and novels which usually incorporated Pan-Africanist themes.

JESSE FAUSET:

was an influential Harlem Renaissance essayist, poetess, novelist, teacher, NAACP and Pan-African activist. As literary editor of the Crisis from 1919 to 1926, she encouraged the careers of several Harlem Renaissance writers, including Countee Cullen, Langston Hughes, Claude McKay, and Jean Toomer. She wrote several novels and many essays which focused on issues of color, women's roles and Pan-Africanism.

*N*egritude

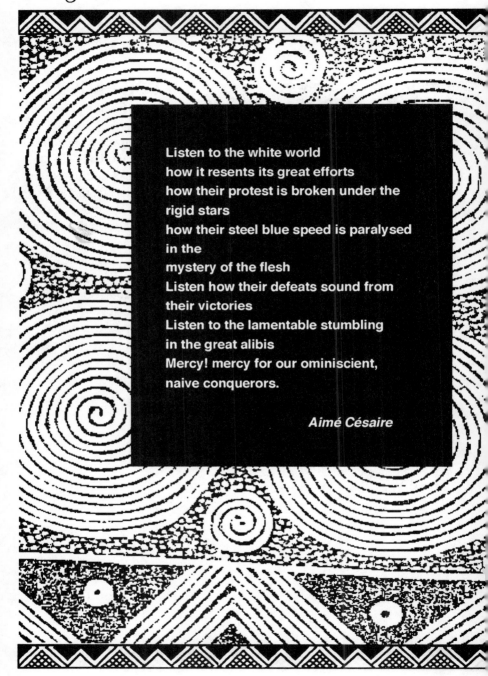

Listen to the white world
how it resents its great efforts
how their protest is broken under the
rigid stars
how their steel blue speed is paralysed
in the
mystery of the flesh
Listen how their defeats sound from
their victories
Listen to the lamentable stumbling
in the great alibis
Mercy! mercy for our ominiscient,
naive conquerors.

Aimé Césaire

There were strong social, psychological and economic ties between the colonial metropole of France, and its African and Caribbean colonies. These ties had their historical roots in the French colonial policy of assimilation. This policy allowed the French colonial government to "**award**" certain African elites **French citizenship**, once they had "**assimilated**" enough "**culture**." Some colonists began to consider themselves "Black Frenchmen," even though they had few of the ascriptive rights of French citizenship. As a reaction, the movement known as **NEGRITUDE** began among African and Caribbean students studying in Paris during the 1930's. The most famous of these students, **AIME CESAIRE (1913-), LEON DAMAS** (1912-1978),

and LEOPOLD SENGHOR (1906-), used poetry to explore their differences and similarities as Blacks. Eventually, Negritude turned into a philosophical criticism of colonialism and a rationale for African Nationalism.

† **N**egritude was the recognition of a distinct African personality found in everyone of African ancestry. One might expect that a movement stressing the existence of an African personality, and justifying African Independence, would have loosened the bond between metropole and colony — but this was not necessarily the case.

† **As FRANZ FANON (1925-61) described them, they had Black skins and white masks. The Negritude movement influenced many of the French-speaking African and Caribbeans who went on to become members of the political elite.**

The philosophy of Negritude was contradictory. It accepted and rejected both African and Western culture. Its followers were in a sense "hybrids" in their view of African culture — part African, part European. Thus, while glorifying "Africaness," there remained a deep psycho-social (and as we will see politico-economic) attachment to France.

FRANZ FANON:

was born in Martinique and educated in France. After completing his medical and psychiatric studies he went to Algeria to work, but soon joined the Algerian armed struggle against French colonialism. His two major work, *Black Skin, White Mask* (1952) and *The Wretched of the Earth* (1961) dealt with the psychological and physical destruction caused by imperialism, colonialism and racism. His works became an inspiration for the colonial peoples of color the world over struggling to be free.

*E*thiopianism

Missionaries and colonialism usually worked hand in hand. European missionaries converted poor Blacks to Christianity and Eurocentric attitudes, which ultimately paved the way for European colonists. People like Holy Johnson and Bishop **SAMUEL CROWTHER,** even though devout Christians, still experienced racism. Such discrimination led to movements in various parts of Africa (as well as the Diaspora) to Africanize Christian churches. ETHIOPIANISM is the term used to describe this movement.

The Emperial Family of Ethiopia, 1936

Features of Ethiopianism:

1) tried to stop white missionaries from destroying African values.

2) believed that Africa belonged to Africans, and opposed European interference.

3) often resulted in breaks with White Churches.

In the United States:
RICHARD ALLEN (1760-1831), a church minister, broke away from white churches and founded the Bethel African Methodist Episcopal (AME) Church in 1797.

Equator

In Jamaica:
An African-American Baptist preacher, and former slave, founded an "Ethiopian" Baptist Church in 1784. Thereafter, Black Baptists became the spokespersons for the Jamaican masses.

*E*thiopianism and Rastafarianism

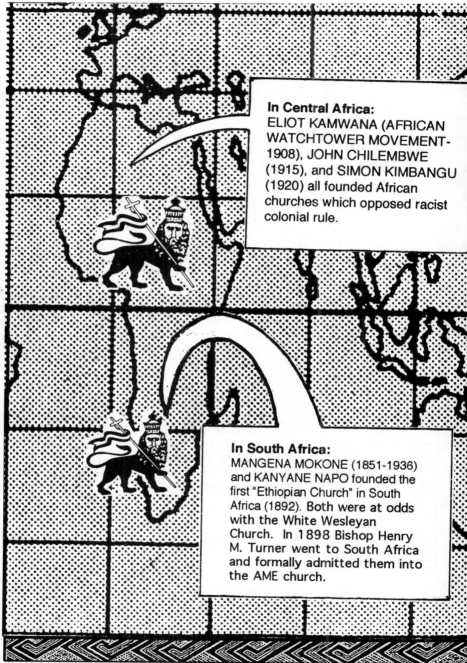

In Central Africa:
ELIOT KAMWANA (AFRICAN WATCHTOWER MOVEMENT-1908), JOHN CHILEMBWE (1915), and SIMON KIMBANGU (1920) all founded African churches which opposed racist colonial rule.

In South Africa:
MANGENA MOKONE (1851-1936) and KANYANE NAPO founded the first "Ethiopian Church" in South Africa (1892). Both were at odds with the White Wesleyan Church. In 1898 Bishop Henry M. Turner went to South Africa and formally admitted them into the AME church.

Throughout the period 1830 to 1930 Black Jamaicans struggled against colonial oppression. In 1916, the Garveys founded the UNIA and preached "Africa for Africans at home and abroad." Marcus Garvey used Ethiopia as a source of inspiration for the liberation of Africans in the Diaspora. His followers viewed Ethiopia as the symbol of freedom from "Babylon" — White Western capitalist society.

Garvey reportedly once said, "look to Africa when a Black King shall be crowned, for the day of deliverance is near." Not long afterwards, in 1928, **RAS TAFARI** (1892-1975) was crowned Emperor **HAILE SELASSIE I** of Abyssinia (Ethiopia). Afterwards many Garvey followers, the most important of which were lay Baptist ministers, began preaching that the "Black King" was divine. Their converts became known as **Rastafarians.**

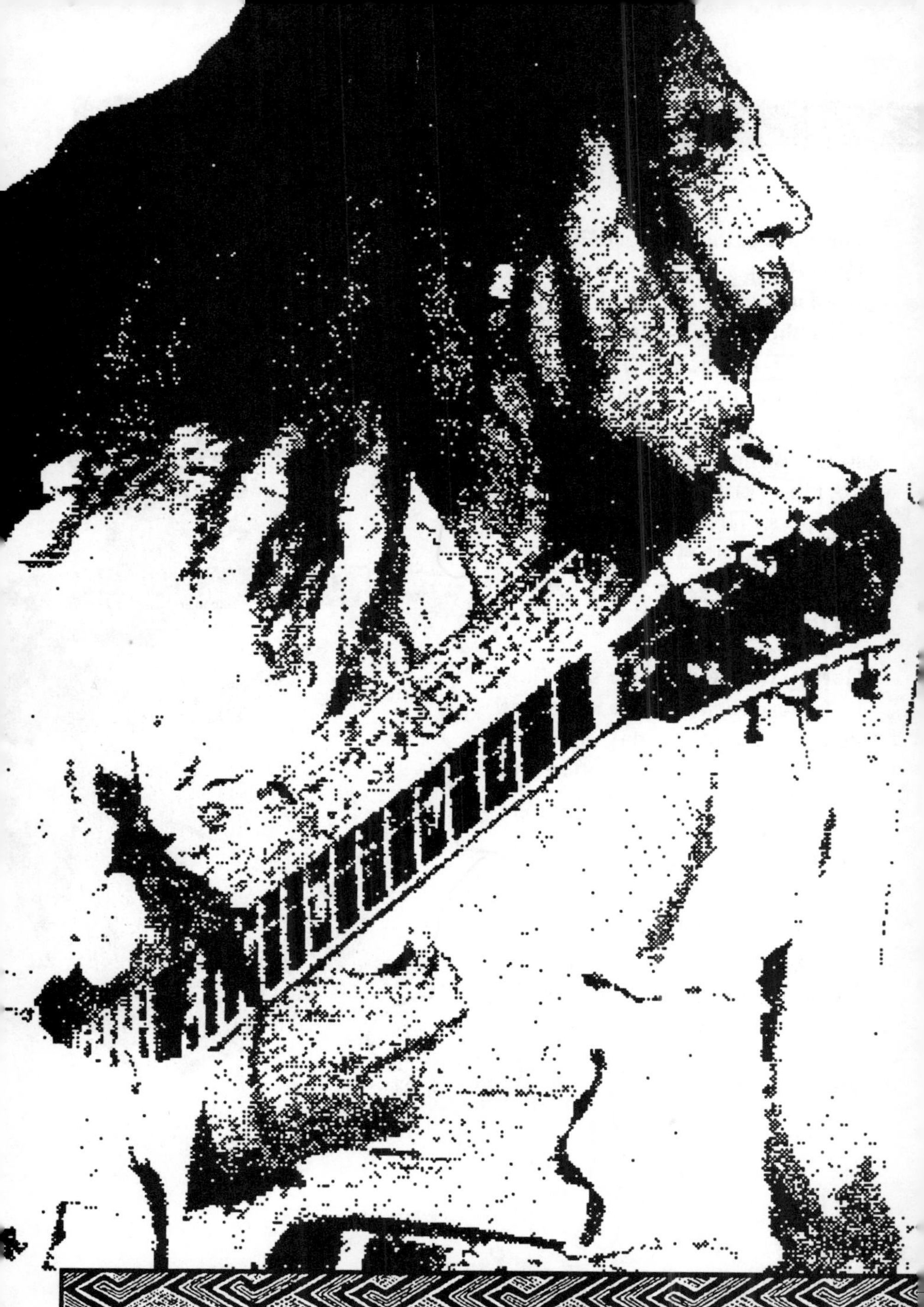

Throughout the years Rastafarianism has retained its connection to Ethiopianism and Garveyism. And, even though it remains a relatively small movement, it has become a cultural vehicle in the struggle for political and economic freedom among Blacks throughout the Diaspora. In Jamaica, Haiti, Zimbabwe and elsewhere in the Diaspora, resistance movements have gathered energy from the Rastafarian popular culture. Not simply for deliverance from "Babylon," but liberation from all oppressors. Through reggae music and films, **"Rastamen"** like Bob Marley...

BOB MARLEY:
(1945-1981) AND THE WAILERS, JIMMY CLIFF, PETER TOSH and others have carried their message of Pan-African unity and resistance around the world.

Get up, stand up

Stand up for your rights

Get up,
stand up

Don't give up
the fight.

Bob Marley and the Wailers

127

The Abyssinian Crisis

In 1935, Italian dictator Benito Mussolini (1883-1945) made preparations to attack and colonize Ethiopia, then known as Abyssinia. In response Africans and diasporans in London formed the **INTERNATIONAL AFRICAN FRIENDS OF ABYSSINIA (IAFA).** Its chair was the distinguished Marxist historian and Pan-African theorist **C.L.R. JAMES (1901-1989)**. The other officials were **Dr. PETER MILLIARD,** (British Guiana), **ALBERT MARRYSHAW, JOMO KENYATTA (Kenya), AMY ASHWOOD GARVEY (Jamaica) and SAMUEL MANNING.** Later another important Pan-Africanist, **GEORGE PADMORE (AKA MALCOLM NURSE(1900-1959),** joined the organization. The IAFA agitated and propagandized against Italian Fascism and colonialism. For them, such threats were yet another potential attack on the "motherland," which they could not let go unchallenged. However, Mussolini took Ethiopia anyway, while the League of Nations looked on meekly.

Since the IAFA had disbanded after white liberals took over the cause, Pan-Africanists formed the INTERNATIONAL AFRICAN SERVICE BUREAU (IASB) to continue the fight. They appealed to Africans and their descendents to join in defending the Ethiopians. They were convinced that a common bond of oppression linked all Black people the world over. They also believed in the need for an international and unified organization to fight for Black rights.

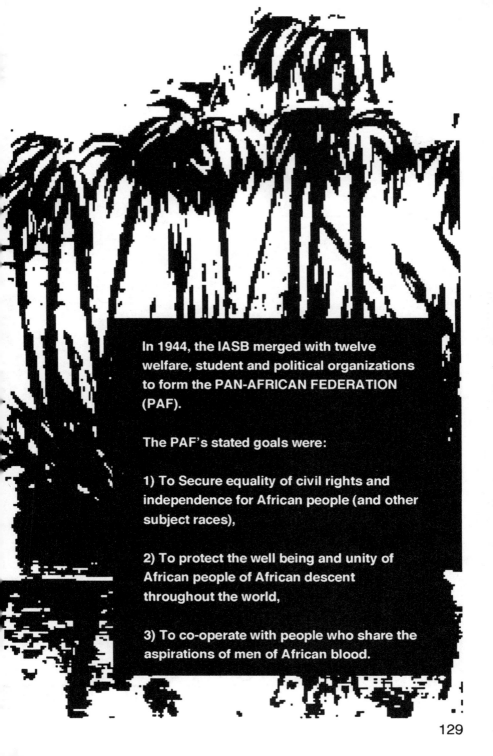

In 1944, the IASB merged with twelve welfare, student and political organizations to form the **PAN-AFRICAN FEDERATION (PAF).**

The PAF's stated goals were:

1) To Secure equality of civil rights and independence for African people (and other subject races),

2) To protect the well being and unity of African people of African descent throughout the world,

3) To co-operate with people who share the aspirations of men of African blood.

C.L.R. JAMES:

was born near Port of Spain, Trinidad in 1901. Following his father, James became a school teacher. He also became an accomplished cricketer and sportsman. James left Trinidad for England in 1932 and began his career as a historian, Pan-Africanist and socialist thinker. Among his many writings was the classic *Black Jacobins*, a marxist history of the Haitian Revolution. His involvement in revolutionary politics had a tremendous influence on many of the African and diasporan leaders who came to power in the 1960's.

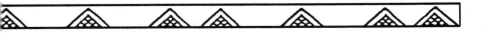

The Fifth Du Bois Pan-African Congress

Also in 1944, The Pan-African Federation made plans
for another Pan-African Congress to coincide with the
British Trade Union Congress (BTUC) to be held the
following year. This would allow them draw in repre-
sentatives of labor organizations from Africa and the
Caribbean.

The Congress organizers included the leaders of the next
generation of Pan-Africanists: Dr. PETER MILLARD of
British Guiana (chair), T.R. MAKONNEN of Ethiopia
(treasurer), GEORGE PADMORE of Trinidad and
KWAME NKRUMAH of the Gold Coast (secretaries),
and JOMO KENYATTA of Kenya (assistant secretary).
The Congress' honorary chair was the "grand old man"
of Pan-Africanism, W.E.B. Du Bois, now seventy-three
years old. It was ironic that the chairperson for the
initial session was AMY ASHWOOD GARVEY, the
first woman chair and former wife of Du Bois' arch-rival
Marcus Garvey.

West African Nationalism

The Fifth Pan African Congress was significant in several important ways. For the first time in the history of the Pan-Africanist movement, Africa was well represented. Furthermore, it was the first time that delegates fully discussed Pan-Africanism and African Nationalism. They emphasized the need for a well organized movement as the only way to win African liberation struggles.

The Congress adopted several resolutions whose aim was to abolish colonial exploitation and injustice. For the first time the Congress demanded "autonomy and independence" for Africa, as well as the right of all colonial peoples to self-determination — i.e. to control their own destiny. Pan-Africanism was no longer simply a protest movement by people of African descent in the Caribbean and the United States; it was becoming a weapon with which African nationalists could fight colonial rule. At its conclusion, the Congress delegates set up a working committee with Du Bois as titular head and Nkrumah as general secretary.

Soon after the Fifth PAC, a group of West African students studying in London set up a WEST AFRICAN NATIONAL SECRETARIAT to put the new Pan-African Nationalism into action.

In 1946 the
Secretariat
convened a
West African
National
Congress to
promote a
West African
Federation —

African Independence and

A first step towards a United States of Africa. This concept bore the distinctive mark of the Congress' chair, Kwame Nkrumah, who later became the leading spokesperson of both Pan-Africanism and African Nationalism.

Pan-Africanism

After the Second Imperialist World War, it became clear to the European colonial powers that direct rule was too costly. They had to find another form of making profits off the colonies. In the late forties and early fifties, Africans stepped up their demands for political independence. Labor strikes, riots and armed struggle were manifestations of this attitude.

In the Gold Coast (Ghana), ex-soldiers rioted at Christianborg; In Senegal, railways workers and market women struck the Dakar-Niger line; in Kenya, peasants and urban workers formed the Land and Freedom Army (which the British called MAU MAU) and took up arms; also in Madagascar and Cameroun peasants wages battles against colonialism.

Thus in the 1950's the "winds of change" blew across the continent, and colonial powers realized that it was only a matter of time before political independence would be granted.

They took two tactics:

1) they create and/or encourage an indigenous governing class that would maintain economic ties to the metropole;

2) they eliminated or neutralized elements within each society that would hinder this relationship.
So began the process of

Decolonization

Kwame Nkrumah served as the link between The Fifth Pan-African Congress, the West African Secretariat and the Independence movement in Africa. He connected his Pan-African background to his later international activities as the first President of Ghana. For Nkrumah, the goal of Pan-Africanism was to go beyond the geographical, national and cultural barriers imposed by colonialism.

In March, 1957 the former Gold Coast colony became the politically independent nation of Ghana. During the celebration, Nkrumah announced that he would call for a conference of the Independent African states to discuss the common problems experienced by the new states.

In 1958, Nkrumah took the lead in calling for the first Conference of Independent African States (CIAS) in Accra. It marked the formal launching of the Pan-African movement on African soil. All eight independent states met, although only four, Ghana, Ethiopia, Sudan and Liberia, belonged to sub-Saharan Africa. The remaining four (Egypt, Tunisia, Libya, and Morocco) were considered Northern African.

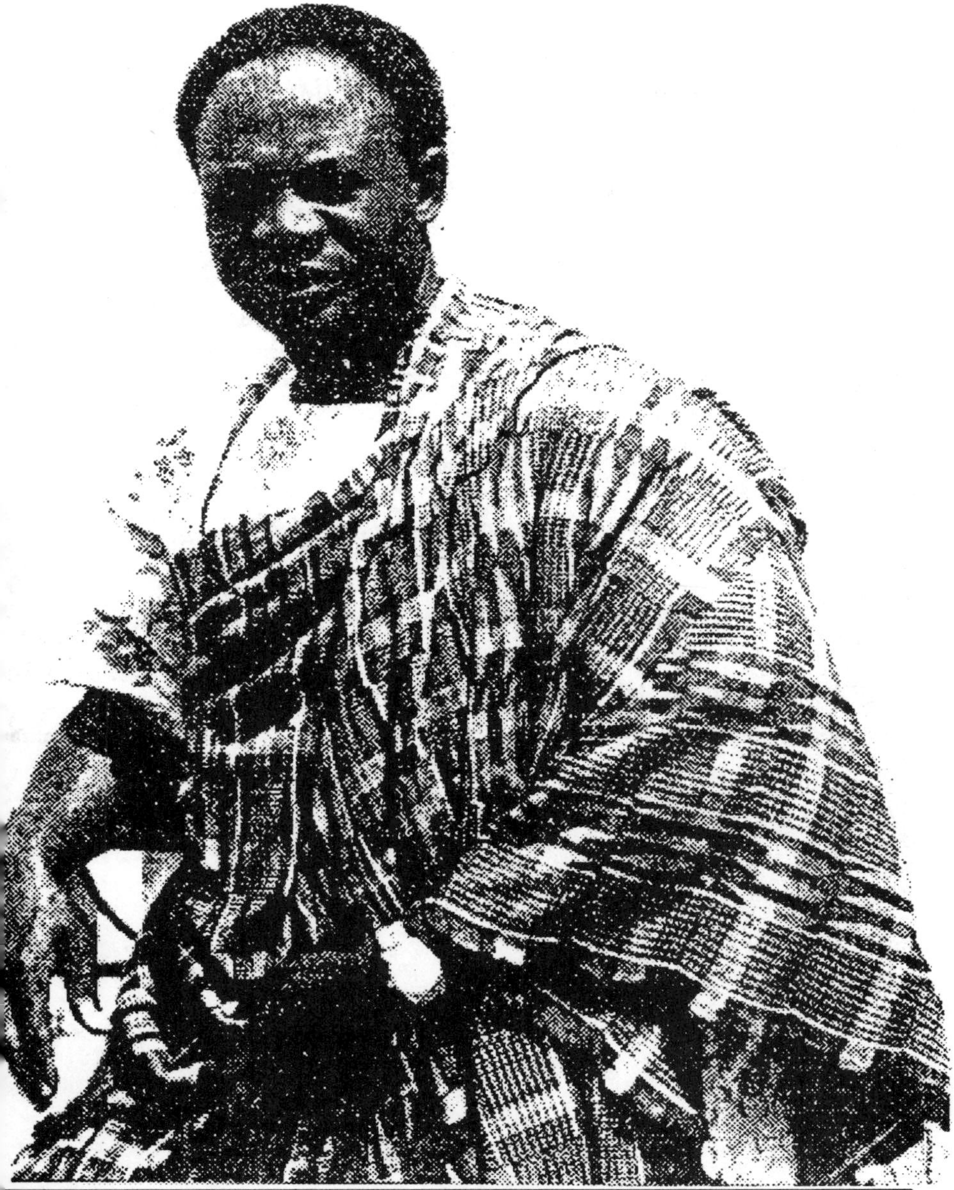

Attempts at Unity

The conference gave a non-voting status to the Algerian Liberation Front (FLN), which was then engaged in armed struggle for Algerian independence from France. Although the FLN presence was later to become a source of friction in the Pan-African movement, the Conference confirmed an important concept of Pan-Africanist philosophy, i.e. a bond existed between the people of Africa. Neither skin color, the Sahara, nor Islam were insurmountable problems to that bond.

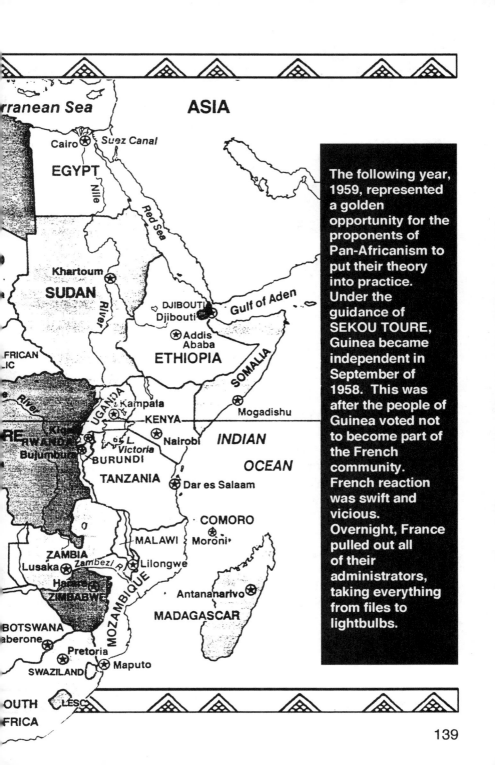

ASIA

rranean Sea

Cairo ⊛ Suez Canal

EGYPT

Nile

Red Sea

Khartoum

SUDAN

River

DJIBOUTI
Djibouti

Gulf of Aden

⊛ Addis
Ababa

ETHIOPIA

SOMALIA

FRICAN
IC

River

UGANDA

Kampala

KENYA

⊛ Nairobi

⊛ Mogadishu

INDIAN

RE
RWANDA
Bujumbura

Kigali
L.
Victoria

BURUNDI

OCEAN

TANZANIA

⊛ Dar es Salaam

COMORO
⊛
Moroni

MALAWI

ZAMBIA
Lusaka ⊛

Zambezi R.

⊛ Lilongwe

Harare ⊛

ZIMBABWE

MOZAMBIQUE

Antananarivo ⊛

MADAGASCAR

BOTSWANA
aberone ⊛

Pretoria ⊛

SWAZILAND

⊛ Maputo

OUTH

LESO

FRICA

The following year, 1959, represented a golden opportunity for the proponents of Pan-Africanism to put their theory into practice. Under the guidance of SEKOU TOURE, Guinea became independent in September of 1958. This was after the people of Guinea voted not to become part of the French community. French reaction was swift and vicious. Overnight, France pulled out all of their administrators, taking everything from files to lightbulbs.

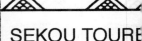
This action almost destroyed Guinea's economic structure.

In response, Ghana immediately came to Guinea's aid. President Toure of Guinea and Nkrumah of Ghana later announced that the two countries would form themselves into a union of West African States. They were to have a common economic, foreign, and defense policy, although each maintained its own army. In May, 1959, Ghana and Guinea agreed to seal the Ghana-Guinea Union with the issuance of the CONAKRY DECLARATION.

Toure and Nkrumah hoped that this would be the beginning of a union of independent African States. Yet, not everyone shared their view. In particular, President WILLIAM TUBMAN (1895-1971) of Liberia felt threatened by the union. He immediately called a meeting with the two heads of state. All three met at Sanniquellie, a small Liberian village in 1959.
The meeting produced the SANIQUELLIE DECLARATION, which formulated principals for the achievement of a Community (no longer a union) of Independent

African States. The Saniquellie Declaration highlighted the friction between Pan-Africanists who wanted a strong political union, and leaders who favored a limited association which protected their power from each other, and from the outside.

Nevertheless, the following year (1960), Nkrumah and Toure joined with President MODIBO KEITA of Mali to form the Ghana-Guinea-Mali Union. Although it soon fell apart, the union was an initial step towards a closer association which influenced African politics.

The Second Conference of Independent African States

In 1960, The Second Conference of Independent African States took place. This conference was significant in two major ways. First, it continued the controversy over the approach towards African unity — i.e. union versus association. Secondly, it showed the cool attitude of African leaders in the French community towards Pan-Africanism.

Although the conveners of the Second CIAS sent invitations to all independent states, only the Algerian provisional government, Cameroon, Ethiopia, Ghana, Guinea, Liberia, Libya, Nigeria, Somolia, Sudan, Tunisia, and the United Arab Republic (Egypt and Syria) attended. The absence of the other states, especially Madagascar, the Mali Federation (Senegal and Mali), Togo — all members of the French African empire — was a storm warning.

*P*an-Africanism and

Given the contradictions inherent in the Negritude philosophy, it is not surprising that before the conference, African leaders in the French Community had shown little or no interest in Nkrumah-style Pan-Africanism.

Now they showed their true allegiance by boycotting the meeting. Their reason: the presence of the provisional government of Algeria at the conference. The only way to understand this situation clearly is to examine the relationship between France and her former French colonies.

The most compelling reason for this clearly contradictory relationship between France and her former colonies was the economic ties which bound them together--which Nkrumah called **NEO-COLONIALISM. President HOUPHOUET-BOIGNY** (1905-?) of the Ivory Coast represents a good example of this relationship. In the early years of Ivory Coast's independence, Boigny sacrificed his country's international political rights by permitting large scale French participation in the Ivory Coast economy.

The advantage was obvious. Such an arrangement insured a continued outflow of capital and maintained relative prosperity. In most of the former French colonies, members of the rich and politically powerful African elites found that they could make money by working together with French capital.

French Neo-Colonialism

This explains the cool attitude of former French colonies towards Algeria and Pan-Africanism — especially Nkrumah's conception of Pan-Africanism. These African elites wanted nothing that would jeopardize their relationship with France and the European economic community.

A United States of Africa

> **Africa will tell the West that today it desires the rehabilitation of Africa, a return to the roots, a revalorization of moral values.**
>
> **The African personality must be expressed...**
> **Africa will have no blocs...**
> **Instead there will be active Africans.**
>
> **Patrice Lumumba**

From the very beginning, Nkrumah spoke of the need for a Unites States of Africa, to rid the continent of colonialism and neo-colonialism. He soon developed many enemies. Nkrumah was just about the only prominent African supporter of political union among African states. Although later, **JULIUS NYERERE (1921-)** of The Republic of Tanzania (a union of Tanganyika and Zanzibar) joined him. Many accused Nkrumah of being a dictator. Others claimed that he was trying to make himself leader of the whole continent. These were the same leaders who could not see a politically united Africa, and were afraid of losing the protection of colonial rule. These Individuals ignored Nkrumah's call for political unity. In affect, Neo-colonial powers used them against Nkrumah. Even though African leaders in the French community were not enthusiastic about Pan-Africanism, they realized that some of its aims were desirable. They understood, for example, that the Pan-African goal of national liberation was worthwhile. They also realized that they must join forces with their fellow states to find solutions to their problems. With the civil war in the **CONGO** where foreign powers (including the C.I.A. and mining companies) aided the Katanga secessionists against **PATRICE LUMUMBA** (1925-1961), no African state could ignore the Pan-African movement.

PATRICE LUMUMBA:

was born in the colony of the Belgium Congo in 1925. His political career began when he was elected president of the African Staff Association at Stanleyville. He developed into a dynamic speaker and propagandist and in 1958 formed the Mouvement National Congolais.(MNC) In June 1960, he became the first Congolese Prime Minister when his country gained independence. Lumumba strongly supported Nkrumah's stance against neo-colonialism, and for Pan-African unity. This frightened the powerful multinational **UNION MINIERE DU HAUTE KATANGA (UMHK)** which (supported by Belgian troops) promptly encouraged the Congo's Katanga province to secede. Lumumba tried to stop the secessionist Tshombe regime but was dismissed by Congolese President Kassavubu. Soon after (February, 1961) he was arrested by some of Tshombes' soldiers, four years later assassinated. With his death, Patrice Lumumba became a Pan-African martyr.

The Brazzaville, Casablanca and Monrovia Groups

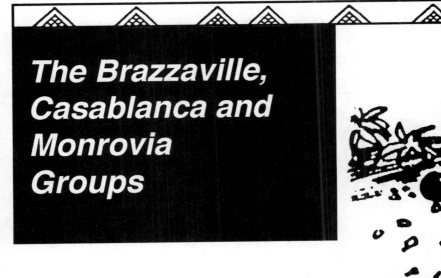

In 1961, independent French-speaking African states called for a meeting at Brazzaville (Congo). The main subject of discussion was the Congo Crisis. After the conference, the participants issued a communique praising the United Nations' action in the Congo. Unfortunately this only added to the disunity within the Pan-African movement.

As a reaction to the Brazzaville conference, another meeting was held in Casablanca (Morocco). This one included African states which were pro-Lumumba and disagreed with United Nations actions in the Congo Crisis. Attending the Casablanca conference were the heads of state of Ghana, Guinea, Mali, Morocco, and the United Arab Republic, plus the Prime Minister of the Algerian provisional government and Libya. From these two meetings the so-called Brazzaville and Casablanca powers evolved.

Although on the surface their disagreements were political and ideological, there was an important underlying factor. The Brazzaville group stood for close and almost exclusive political and economic connection with France, and association with the European economic community.

They argued that economic development required large capital aid from the "First World," which Pan-Africanism and African socialism would frightened away. On the other hand, the Casablanca group rejected this stand. They argued that such "aid" would help meet the immediate needs of the new countries, but would not change the basic exploitative economic relationships with the Capitalist world. They advocated "belt-tightening," a get-tough attitude toward Europe and America, and a common market in Africa.

*P*an-African Regional Movements

As a way out of this impasse, yet another conference was held at Monrovia (Liberia) in 1961. This time all French-speaking states were present, and joined by a majority of the former British colonies (minus the Casablanca group). While some gestures were made towards reconciliation, little of substance came out of the Conference. Although the Monrovia powers did sharply condemn colonialism, they backed away from militant Pan-Africanism.

While the realities of neo-colonialism broke the fragile Pan-African bond, there were several instances in which African leaders showed a degree of cooperation. They created large regional experiments in East, Central and Southern Africa.

In 1958 a group came together at Mwanza, Tanganyika and formed The **PAN-AFRICAN MOVE-MENT FOR EAST AND CENTRAL AFRICA (PAFMECA).** It was an extremely loose grouping of political parties from Tanganyika,

Kenya, Uganda, Northern and Southern Rhodesia, Nyasaland and Zanzibar. **PAFMECA,** a brainchild of Julius Nyerere, was the only effective regional political organization on the continent. It acted as a coordinating body, rather than as a unifying organization. Yet, despite some divisions, it achieved a remarkable (although temporary) degree of unity on major questions.

At its third annual conference, PAFMECA considered plans for an East African Federation of Kenya, Tanganyika, Uganda and Zanzibar after all became independent. The federation was to be a first and logical step towards the final goal of total African unity. Later, delegates from African parties in Basutoland (Lesotho), Bechuanaland (Botswana), South Africa, South West Africa (Namibia), and Swaziland joined. They became The PAN AFRICAN MOVEMENT OF EASTERN, CENTRAL AND SOUTHERN AFRICA (PAFMECSA). However, the group disbanded in 1963, after the Organization of African Unity (OAU) was founded.

*T*he Organization of African Unity

In 1963 African nations set up the **ORGANIZATION OF AFRICAN UNITY (OAU)** in Addis Ababa, Ethiopia. In its early years, the OAU had some impact in both international and domestic spheres.

In the UN, it exerted influence on fellow member states to ostracize apartheid South Africa and Portugal in the early 1960's. The OAU also played a role in mediating several disputes among African states. However, the OAU has experienced more failures than successes in African affairs. Some of these setbacks were unimportant, but others were major and are still having important effects. These incidents included the inability of the OAU to achieve the liberation of South Africa and to deal with the neo-colonial economic structures built by imperialism during the decolonization period.

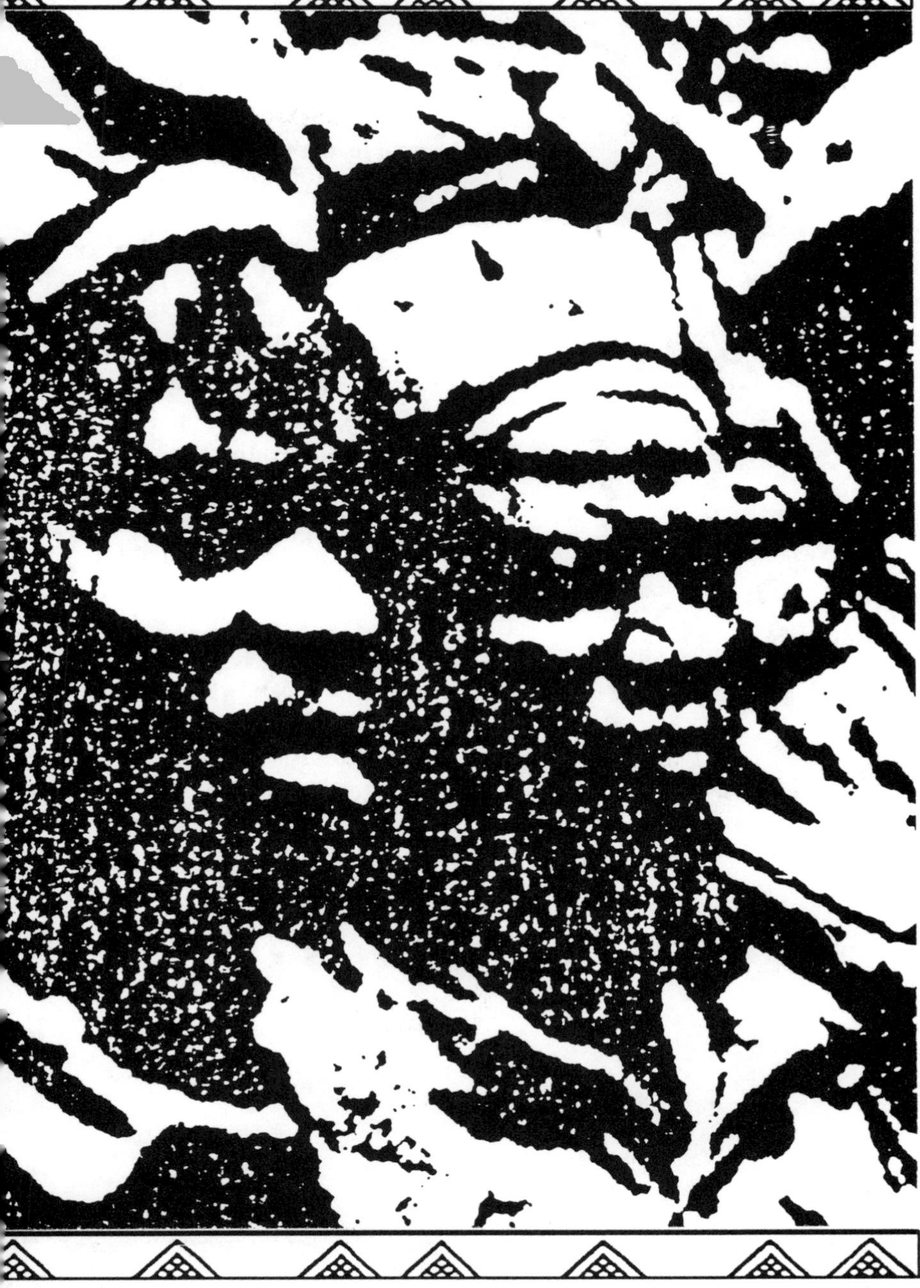

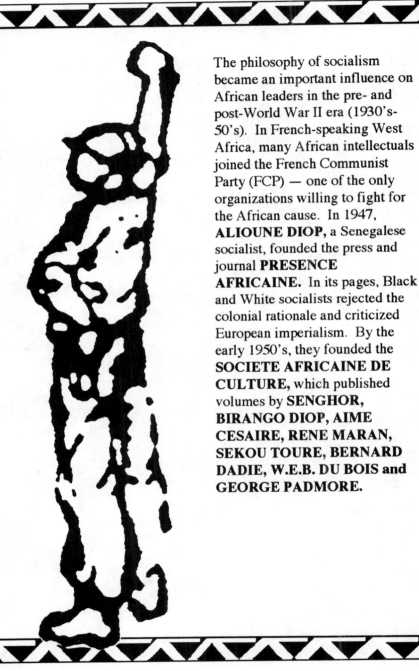

The philosophy of socialism became an important influence on African leaders in the pre- and post-World War II era (1930's-50's). In French-speaking West Africa, many African intellectuals joined the French Communist Party (FCP) — one of the only organizations willing to fight for the African cause. In 1947, **ALIOUNE DIOP,** a Senegalese socialist, founded the press and journal **PRESENCE AFRICAINE.** In its pages, Black and White socialists rejected the colonial rationale and criticized European imperialism. By the early 1950's, they founded the **SOCIETE AFRICAINE DE CULTURE,** which published volumes by **SENGHOR, BIRANGO DIOP, AIME CESAIRE, RENE MARAN, SEKOU TOURE, BERNARD DADIE, W.E.B. DU BOIS and GEORGE PADMORE.**

In addition, they published works by the influential Senegalese socialist **CHIEKH ANTA DIOP.** His *Nations Negres et Culture* [Black Nations and Culture], stressed Black contributions to civilization particularly Ancient Egypt.

African political leaders like Nkrumah, Toure, Nyerere, Kaunda and Senghor embraced certain socialist principles, as a way of building people's democracies. In later years, other leaders such as **EDOUARDO MANDALAND, AMILCAR CABRAL, SAMORA MICHEL, AUGUSTINO NETO, SAM NJOMA, ROBERT MUGABE and NELSON MANDELA** all (to varying degrees) used socialist ideology as the philosophical foundation of their respective liberation movements.

VIVA O MARXISMO-LENINISMO

SIGAMOS o EXEMPL
HERÓIC

While African Socialism accepts certain tenants of
Pan-Africanism (particularly nationalists elements)
and Socialism (especially the co-operative aspects), it
rejects others. For instance, it ignores one of the main
aspects of marxist socialism — the class struggle.
African Socialism's focus on internal political and
economic problems associated with development has
not enabled it to break neo-colonial /imperialist ties.
In fact, many critics on the left question whether
African Socialism, in its various forms, even exists.
They argue that it often bears more resemblance to
LEFT-WING NATIONALISM and UTOPIANISM
than Socialism (or even radical Pan-Africanism).

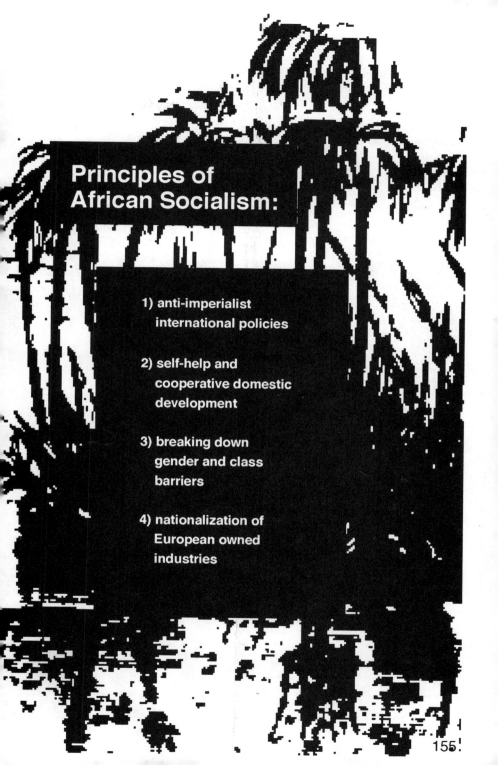

Principles of
African Socialism:

1) anti-imperialist
   international policies

2) self-help and
   cooperative domestic
   development

3) breaking down
   gender and class
   barriers

4) nationalization of
   European owned
   industries

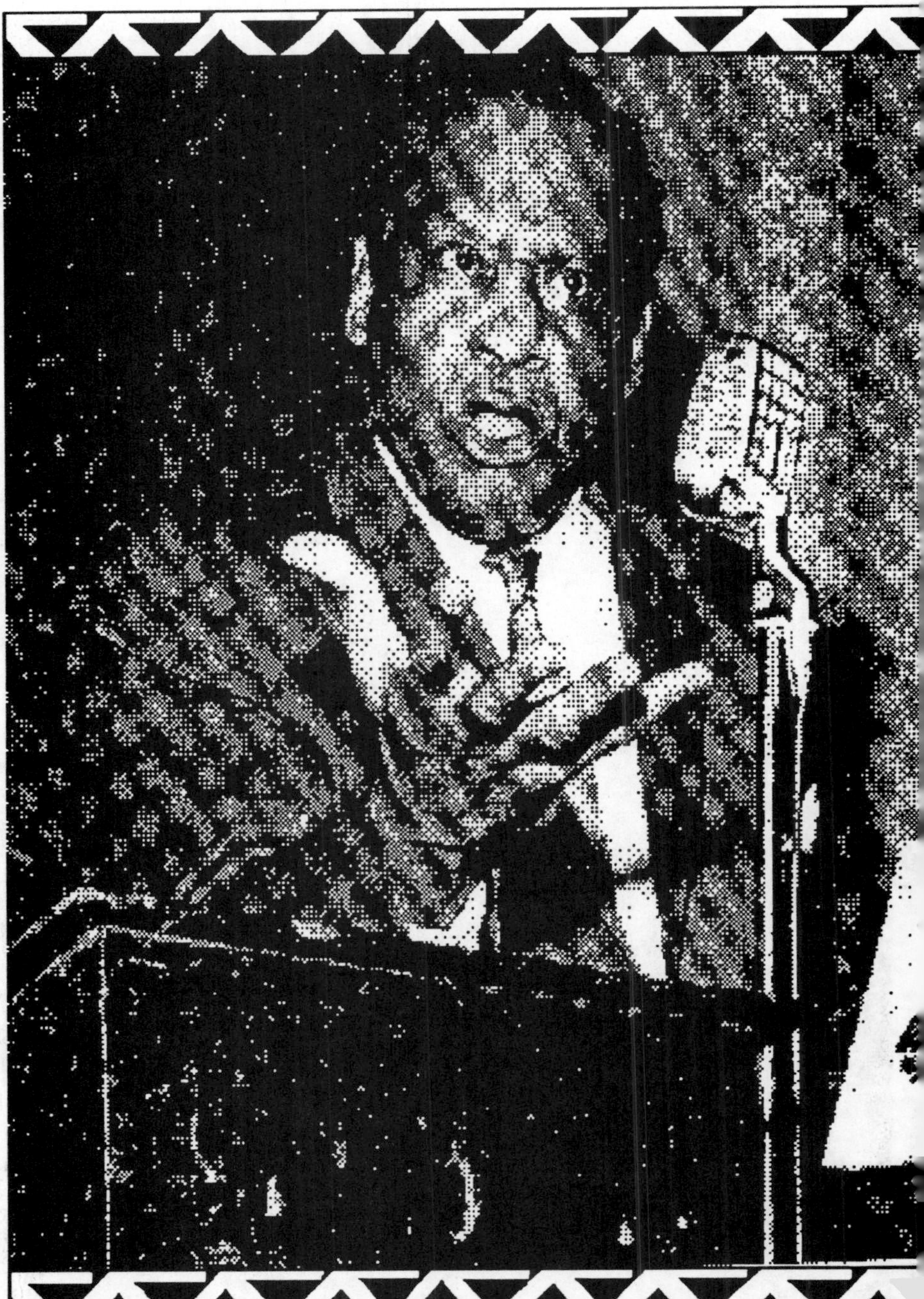

*I think a good deal in terms
of the power of the black people in the
world. That's why
Africa means so much to me.*

*As an American Negro,
I'm as proud of Africa...
spiritually I've been
a part of Africa for a long time.*

Yes, this black power moves me.

Paul Robeson

BLACK
CONSCIOUSNESS

AND
BLACK POWER

The period after the Second World War saw African-Americans step up the struggle for dignity and equality. Encouraged by several favorable Supreme Court decisions on education and segregation, Blacks demanded their civil and human rights. Leaders like Paul Robeson (1898-1976), Ralph Bunche (1900-1974) and Martin Luther King, Jr. (1929-68) helped the Civil Rights Movement pick up steam. Yet by the 1960's, many African-Americans, frustrated by the slow pace of the Civil Rights Movement, took to the streets in Black ghettoes across the U.S. Places like Watts, Harlem and Detroit were scenes of popular rebellions.

In the sixties, Black people looked for answers to their continuing oppression and exclusion from American society.

One person who provided some vision and understanding was **MALCOLM X** (1925-1965). His militant message incorporated much of the Pan-Africanist philosophy and fed into the growing **BLACK CONSCIOUSNESS** movement. Young disciples of Malcolm's legacy formed militant organizations to continue the fight.

STOKLEY CARMICHAEL (KWAME TOURE) and H. RAP BROWN of the STUDENT NONVIOLENT COORDINATING COMMITTEE (SNCC), JAMES FARMER of the CONGRESS OF RACIAL EQUALITY (CORE), HUEY P. NEWTON, BOBBY SEALS, ELDRIDGE CLEAVER, ASSATA SHAKUR, ELAINE BROWN and FRED HAMPTON of the BLACK PANTHERS PARTY, ANGELA DAVIS of the Communist Party (USA) and others became conscious of their "Blackness" and African roots. They promoted African-American and African History as a means of empowering Black people to demand self-determination, that is, to demand the right to control their own destiny. They used the term **BLACK POWER** to reflect that desire.

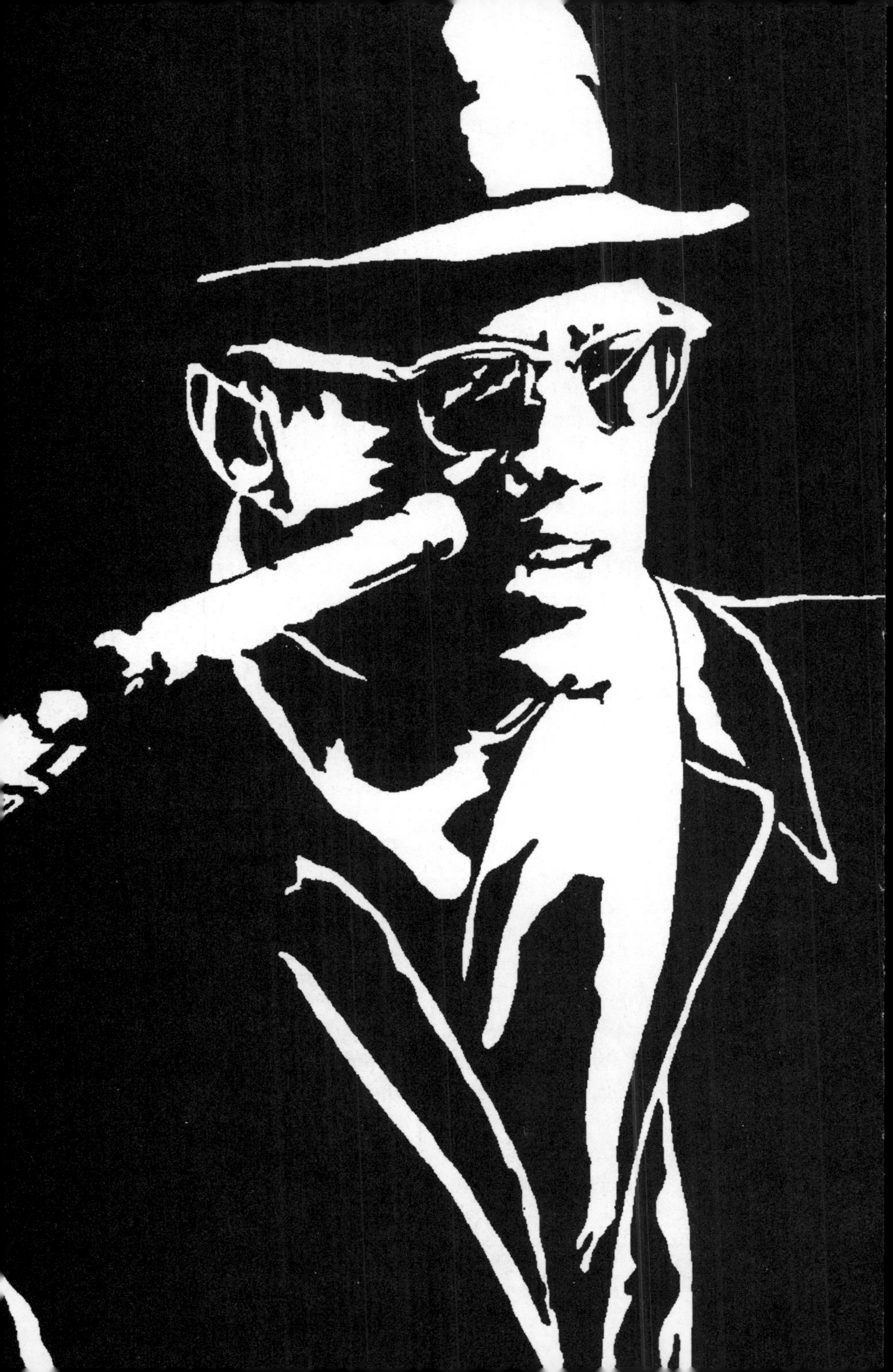

MALCOLM X:

Was born Malcolm Little in 1925. His father, a follower of Marcus Garvey, was lynched by a white mob when Malcolm was still a child. He lived with various family members, but drifted into a life of crime and drugs. Eventually, Malcolm ended up in jail where he first came under the influence of ELIJAH MUHAMMAD (1897-1975), leader of the BLACK MUSLIMS. Upon his release from prison, he became the spokesperson for the movement and quickly gained national and international prominence. He left the Muslims and formed the ORGANIZATION OF AFRO-AMERICAN UNITY to continue his fight. In 1963 he made two trips to Africa and met with many heads of state. In his last years, Malcolm broadened his Black nationalism and became an internationalist — linking the struggle of Black people in Africa and the diaspora against the common enemy of Imperialism.

Although he was assassinated in 1965, his influence remains until today.

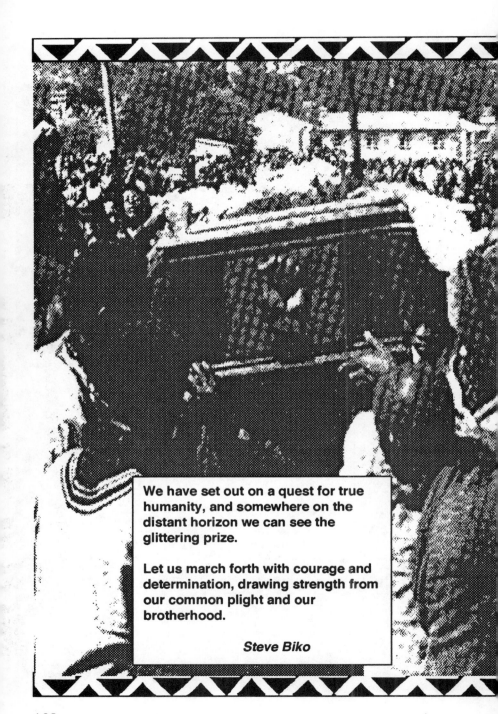

We have set out on a quest for true humanity, and somewhere on the distant horizon we can see the glittering prize.

Let us march forth with courage and determination, drawing strength from our common plight and our brotherhood.

Steve Biko

Black Consciousness, as developed in the United States, influenced movements in other areas of the Black world. **STEVEN BANTU BIKO** (1946-1977), a Black South African militant, used the ideology to "**consciencize**" his people about apartheid. Inside South Africa, he kept the struggle alive which banned groups like the **AFRICAN NATIONAL CONGRESS (ANC) and the PAN-AFRICANIST CONGRESS** (PAC), which had begun in the 1950's. Biko and members of the **BLACK CONSCIOUSNESS MOVEMENT (BCM)** focused their activities on reviving self-dignity and confidence among Black South Africans, who had been victimized by racist apartheid policies.

As is so often the case, reality subordinates a dream. Such was the case with Pan-Africanism. The reality of the independence struggles on the African continent subordinated the dream of a union of Africans and the African Diaspora. However, with the social and political upheaval of the sixties and seventies, Blacks in the Caribbean and the Americas again looked to Africa. Many Diasporan Blacks felt that since Africa was now independent, she should return the favor to those who had helped in that liberation process. They felt a need to redefine and redirect the Pan African movement.

In 1974 the SIXTH PAN AFRICAN CONGRESS was held in Dar es Salaam, Tanzania. President Julius Nyerere hosted the meeting. In attendance were over 500 delegates (representing 52 delegations) from all over the African Diaspora. The Congress represented another transitional stage in the Pan African movement. From the opening speeches by Nyerere and Toure, to the papers presented

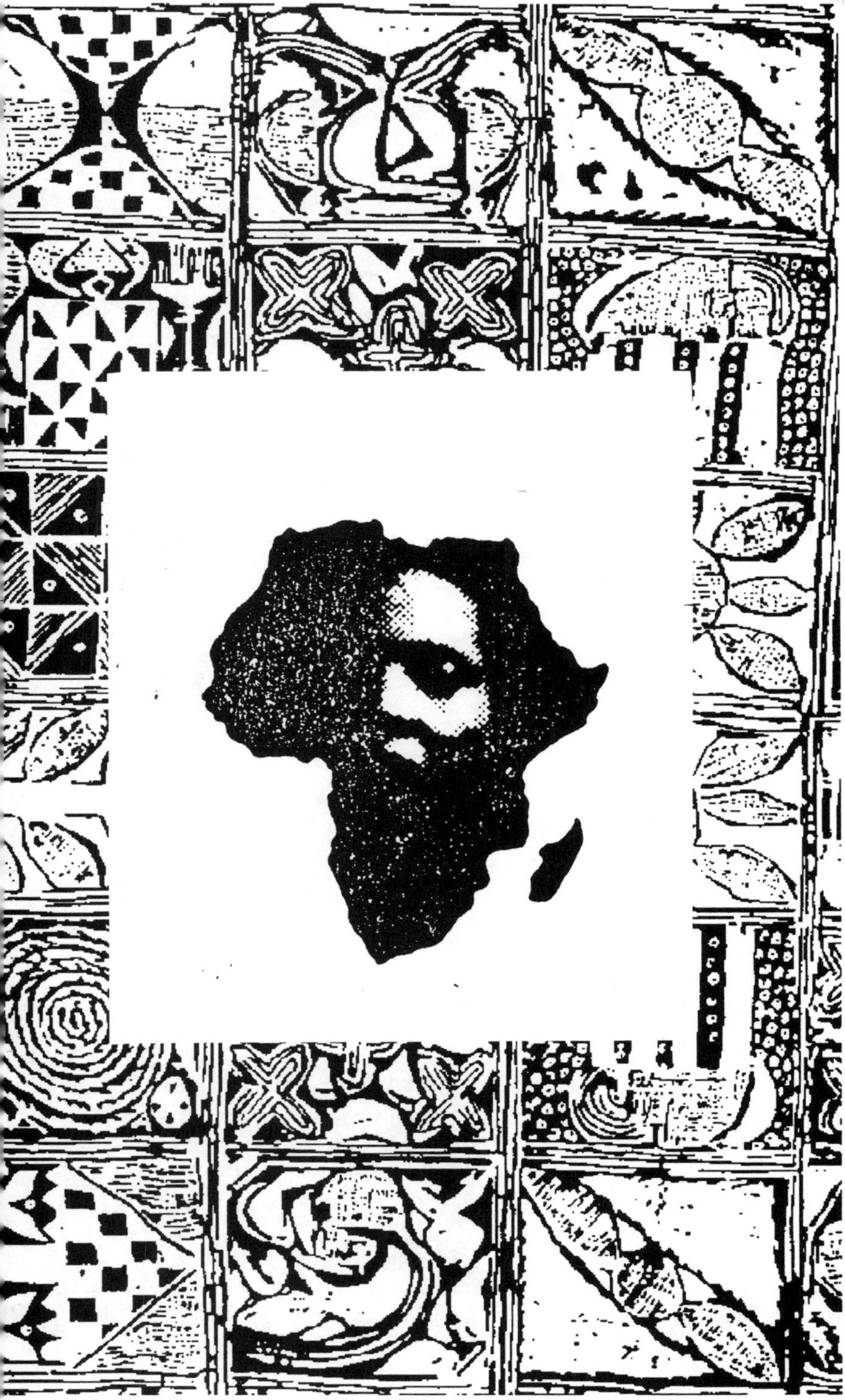

by **WALTER RODNEY, IMAMU BARAKA, FRELIMO, SWAPO, ANC, PLO** and other liberation movements, there was an attempt to link the struggles of African peoples and the African Diaspora with the struggles of other third world peoples. The key question they all wrestled with: What is the place of Pan-Africanism in the changing political arena of 1974?

When the Congress ended, many felt that it was an all important first step in reviving and pushing forward the movement. Others, however, felt it was an ideological and political disaster that endangered the future of Pan-Africanism. For them, the illusory gains of independence and cooperation which characterizes the Pan-Africanist movement in the sixties and early seventies were replaced by political division and economic strife in the late seventies (and eighties). Pan-Africanism had became a concept and a movement which was rapidly decreasing in significance. In many ways these perspectives epitomizes the historical contradictions of the movement.

WALTER RODNEY:

was born on **March 23, 1942** in Georgetown, **Guyana.** After winning a scholarship in 1960, he attended the University of the West Indies (UWI) in Jamaica. From there he travelled to England to study at the School of Oriental and African Studies. **At age 24** he received his **doctorate with honors**. He taught for many years at the University of Dar es Salaam and for a year at U.W.I. During this period he became a renowned **Marxist historian** and one of the foremost spokespersons for Pan-Africanism. In 1974, Rodney returned to Guyana and became active in the **Working People's Alliance,** a militant political party. After being arrested several times on trumped up charges, on **June 13, 1980** he was **assassinated**. As with many other Pan-Africanists he paid for his beliefs with his life, but also managed to influence many of his generation — and after.

In the current climate of racial tensions, crumbling economic systems and reemerging nationalism, many have again questioned the importance of the Pan-African phenomenon. However, there are those in Africa and the Diaspora who still believe in the viability of the idea.

Black struggles in South Africa intensified in the seventies with the Soweto Rebellion (1976), the assassination of anti-apartheid activists like Steve Biko (1977), and the continuing policy of segregation and oppression. In the 1980's, this resulted in a campaign among Diasporans to undermine the economic base of Apartheid through **DIVESTMENT.** The aim of the campaign was to force American individuals and institution to withdraw their investment (divestment) from companies doing business in South Africa.In cities throughout the United States and Europe, Blacks and Whites called for divestment and an end to the Apartheid regime in South Africa.

Contradictions in the Movement

The Pan-African movement, in its various political and cultural manifestations, was at base a reaction to Western Imperialism and cultural hegemony. As Walter Rodney pointed out in his brilliant paper at the Sixth PAC, class contradictions also produced contradictions in the Pan-African movement. The same Black people who helped fuel Pan-Africanism were effectively marginalized from the political and economic systems they knew and valued in their own countries. They directed their anger and frustration against the political and cultural injustices of Western Civilization, yet only a few intellectuals attacked the economic aspects of European and American Imperialism. Most Blacks wanted a peaceful world in which all people of African descent could enjoy full political rights, yet they were unable to see that capitalism and its' class agents (both white and black) have blocked that realization. The erroneous unstated assumption of the movement was that all Black people shared a common class perspective and position within the dominant society. Although these contradictions continued, and lead to further divisions and misplaced emphasis within the Pan-African movement, there is a bright ray of hope on the horizon.

In 1988, under pressure from the U.S. CONGRESSIONAL BLACK CAUCUS and individuals like JESSE JACKSON (Rainbow Coalition) and RANDALL ROBINSON (TransAfrica), the U.S. Senate imposed sanctions against South Africa. They also combined with other anti-apartheid groups around the world to pushed for, and eventually win, independence for Namibia and the release of political prisoners like Nelson Mandela, Walter Sisulu and others (although many others remain).

Upon his release from prison Mandela made a worldwide tour and was cheered by millions of supporters. This reception re-emphasized the Pan-African commitment of solidarity with Black South Africans in their struggle for freedom. Even though President Bush lifted U.S. sanctions in 1991 (claiming that "irreversible progress" had been made) Apartheid still exists — but its days are numbered.

As we enter the nineties, we should see the struggle against Apartheid as a new stage in the development of Pan-Africanism — an international reawakening. Jesse Jackson and others have placed on the national and international agenda the importance of Blacks rediscovering and reaffirming their cultural, historical and political links with Africa. The exact form this renewed Pan-Africanism will take is uncertain.

However, one thing is for sure, as long as Black people around the world continue to face oppression and exploitation, the idea of Pan-Africanism will continue to exist — and the struggle will continue.

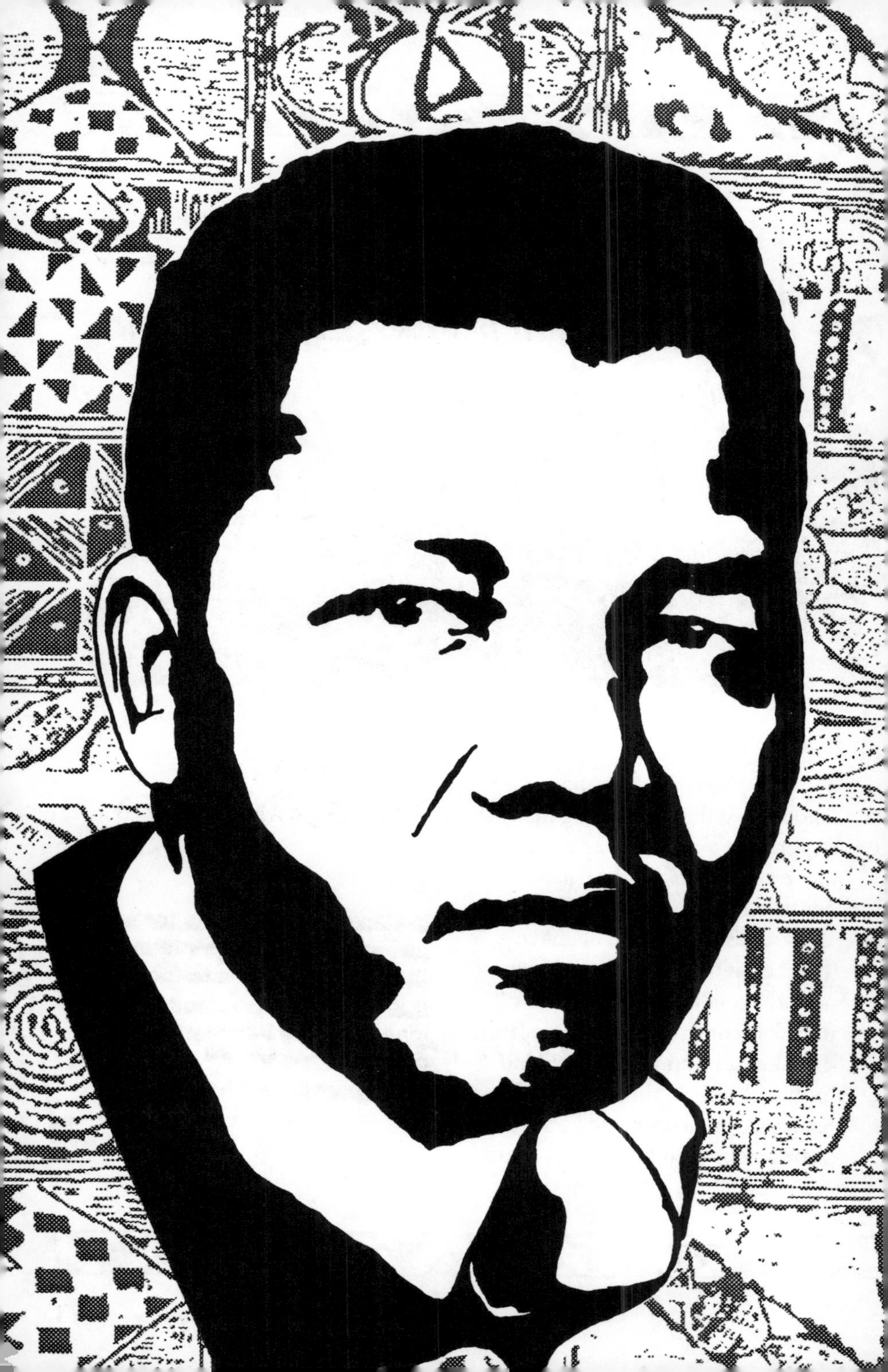

*During my lifetime I dedicated
myself to this struggle of the
African people. I have fought
against white domination.
I have cherished the ideal of a
democratic society in which
all persons live together in
harmony, and with equal
opportunities. It is an ideal
which I hope to live for and
achieve. But, if need be,
it is an ideal for which I am
prepared to die.*

Nelson Mandela

GLOSSARY

AFRICA FOR THE AFRICAN: A slogan and movement closely associated with Ethiopianism and Garveyism (often referred to as the Back to Africa Movement). The phrase was first used in 1861 by the Black American abolitionist, Dr. Martin R. Delany (1812-1885), who planned to resettle African-Americans in Africa. [Delany, in his early career as an abolitionist and fighter for the rights of African-Americans, wanted Blacks to remain in the U.S. and demand their rights as citizens. After 1853 he changed his mind and began supporting emigration to Latin America and Africa.] The slogan "Africa for the African" was also used by the Liberian Pan-Africanist E. W. Blyden (1832-1912) and others in the 19th century. However, it became most popular in the 1920's among Marcus Garvey (1887-1940) and his followers. [see GARVEYISM and ETHIOPIANISM]

AFRICAN NATIONALISM: see NATIONALISM.

AFRICAN NATIONAL CONGRESS (ANC): A multi-racial (although principally Black) anti-apartheid organization originally formed in 1912 as the South African Native National Congress. In its early years the group was primarily made up of European and American educated Black South Africans who wanted better treatment from the government. In 1923 the group changed its name, dropping the derogatory term "Native" for the more acceptable "African." In the 1940's and 50's the ANC became more militant, leading strikes and demonstrations against the Apartheid system. In 1960's the White South African government banned the group because of its "subversive" activities. In 1990, after thirty one years of underground struggle, the ANC was unbanned and, under its leader Nelson Mandela, continues the struggle for a free South Africa. [see also APARTHEID, BLACK CONSCIOUSNESS, and PAN-AFRICAN CONGRESS]

AFRICAN PERSONALITY: An idea which maintains that Africans and people of African descent possess a distinct personality/psyche based on shared experiences, customs and spiritual values. The term was first used in 1881 by E.W. Blyden. He subsequently developed the notion in a series of lectures and articles. It was later elaborated upon by Marcus Garvey (1920's) and Kwame Nkrumah (1960's). Many writers use the terms African Personality, Pan-Africanism and Negritude synonymously, although important political and economic differences exist between them. [see NEGRITUDE]

AFRICAN SOCIALISM: see SOCIALISM

APARTHEID: The system of discrimination and racial segregation practiced by the white Afrikaner government against Black South Africans. The word apartheid is Afrikaans (language spoken by white South Africans of Dutch descent who arrived at Cape town in 1652) for "apartness." Originally it reflected the Afrikaner attitude towards the British who captured Cape Colony in 1795. The Afrikaners viewed the British as imperialist exploiters and wanted to be apart from them. However, Apartheid, as a set of discriminatory and exploitative practices against Africans, existed from the 18th century. Its main purpose was to control the essential commodity of African labor (particularly for the gold and diamond mines). In 1910, with the formation of the Union of South Africa (USA), Apartheid-type laws were set up. (Most were modeled after the 19th century Black codes and segregation laws of the U.S.) Later, after the election of 1948, Apartheid became the official policy of the ruling Afrikaner Nationalist Party. It is composed of a series laws and policies which denied Black South Africans their basic human rights (citizenship, voting, freedom of movement

and residence etc). While many of the original Apartheid laws were repealed in 1991, Blacks (which, contrary to government attempts to artificially divide South Africans along race/color/"tribal" lines, includes indigenous Africans, those of Indians ancestry and those of mixed ancestry or so-called "Coloureds") still are denied their basic rights. [see also ANC, BLACK CONSCIOUSNESS and PAN-AFRICAN CONGRESS]

BLACK CONSCIOUSNESS: A concept and a movement among Blacks which stressed self-awareness and knowledge of African and Afro-American history. The desire to rediscover and become aware/conscious of their African heritage resulted from the conditions under which Blacks lived. In the United States, these ideas arose throughout the period of slavery and after. In the 1960's, in the wake of the Civil Rights and Black Power Movements (and ghetto rebellions in most major cities), this sentiment was revived in the term Black Consciousness. It became popular among young African-Americans struggling against oppression in White-American society. They rejected the old term "Negro" (which was equated with being submissive and compliant — i.e. an "Uncle Tom") and instead called themselves Black or Afro-American. A related movement developed in South Africa in the wake of the 1976 Soweto Rebellion. Its prime organizer was Steve Biko (1946-1977), a former Black medical student. Biko and others seized on the idea of Black Consciousness as a way to combat the racist apartheid system of segregation. In the 1970's they formed the *BLACK CONSCIOUSNESS MOVEMENT* (BCM), a federation of many local and national groups bound together by the concept of Black consciousness. BCM became involved in education and community action campaigns designed to build self-respect and self-reliance.[see BLACK POWER and APARTHEID].

BLACK MUSLIMS: see NATION OF ISLAM.

BLACK NATIONALISM: see NATIONALISM.

BLACK PANTHER PARTY: see BLACK POWER.

BLACK POWER: A slogan, concept and movement of the late 1960's. Even though the term was used by people like Richard Wright and Adam Clayton Powell Jr. more than a decade earlier, the individuals most associated with it were SNCC activists Willie Ricks and Stokley Carmichael. [The latter, along with Charles V. Hamilton, wrote the 1967 book *Black Power*.] During a civil rights march in 1966, Ricks began to use the slogan "Black Power" (much to the dismay of Martin Luther King, who thought it would scare White supporters). Thereafter, it became a catch-phrase for more militant Blacks, most of whom had been influenced by Malcolm X. While few agreed on an exact definition of the term, Black Power came to symbolize a desire by Black people to control their own destiny. In political terms, it meant Black people uniting and having the voting power to elect representative officials. In cultural terms, it reflected racial pride — captured in the phrase "Black is Beautiful." In economic terms, it meant recognizing how capitalism oppressed Black Americans, as well as people of color in the "Third World." By 1968 Black Power had become the dominant ideology among militant Black youth in the U.S. and Britain. The Black Panther Party, formed in 1966 by Huey P. Newton and Bobby Seale, epitomized the transition from the Civil Rights movement to the Black Power movement. Yet, from its beginning until its decline in the mid-1970's, Black Power was not a consistent ideology or program supported by all activists. [see BLACK CONSCIOUSNESS, NATIONALISM and SELF-DETERMINATION]

CHAUVINISM: was adopted from the name Nicolas Chauvin, a French soldier and diplomat during the time of Napoleon I. Chauvin was a fanatical patriot who believed that French language and culture were superior to any on earth (specifically Europeans, since those outside Europe did not even qualify as "civilized humans"). In the 19th century the term became synonymous with extreme French Nationalism, but later applied to any form of nationalism. From this derived the term *WHITE CHAUVINISM,* which denotes those who have a sense of superiority about White people — i.e. a form of racism. MALE CHAUVINISM is a similar term with reference to male superiority (as in male chauvinist pig). [see also NATIONALISM].

CULTURAL NATIONALISM: see NATIONALISM.

DIASPORA: derives from a Greek word meaning "a scattering." Originally it referred specifically to the scattering of the Jews after expulsion from Babylon. In the 1950's and 1960's (the period of African political Independence) the term AFRICAN DIASPORA was applied to Africans and their descendants scattered around the globe—the result of European capitalist greed for African slave labor and nationalist/imperialist wars in the 19th and 20th centuries. Yet, while the term African Diaspora is of fairly recent origin, the concept of African dispersal and return goes back to the 19th century works of E. W. Blyden, William Wells Brown (1816-1884) and others. [NOTE: In the context of this book the word DIASPORAN designates a person of African descent in the "New World" and Europe.

DIVESTMENT: A campaign, first begun in the 1960's (after Sharpville Massacre), which encourages companies and banks doing business in

forcing the White Afrikaner government to abolish apartheid and institute a policy of majority rule.

ETHIOPIANISM: An early form of Pan-Africanism (and African Nationalism) which was derived form the term "Ethiopia" — (from AITHO = burn or shine, and OP = face) the Greek word for Africa used in the bible. Ethiopianism was a church-based ideology developed by African and African-American ministers who were victims of segregation and racism in White churches. In forming their own "Ethiopian" or "African" (as in African Methodist Episcopal) churches, these Black ministers broke with White churches. By doing so, they tried to save African values from destruction by White missionaries, while salvaging aspects of Christianity from its inherent contradictions. They believed that Africa belonged to Africans, and opposed European interference in African affairs, especially religion. In some ways, Garveyism secularized Ethiopianism in the twenties.

EUROCENTRISM: An ideology which argues that Europe and the European cultural heritage is superior to any on earth [literally that Europe is the center around which every other continent revolves]. In the age of imperialism, Eurocentrism justified the forceful domination of European nations in the "third world," and the hegemony of Western culture. [see CHAUVINISM, SOCIAL DARWINISM and RACISM]

FASCISM: [From the word <u>fasces</u> - rods tied around an ax which was the symbol of authority for Roman magistrates — later became the symbol of Italian fascists or the *Fascisti*. Often Fascism is incorrectly termed "National" Socialism but actually is a violent form of nationalism.] A set of nationalist and racist government doctrines which characterized Fascist Italy (and Nazi

Germany). Fascism, first instituted in Italy in 1922, used force to protect the interests of the Italian capitalist class. The fascist state brutally suppressed any opposition group (particularly leftist parties, unions, ethnic minorities (Jews etc.) which posed a threat to their domination. In 1935, Fascist dictator Benito Mussolini (1883-1945) invaded Abyssinia (Ethiopia), which set off a worldwide movement by Pan-Africanists to oust the Italian invaders. With the defeat of Fascism in the Second Imperialism World War, Ethiopia regained its independence (1941). However, Fascism, as a doctrine of racist and corporate domination, is still with us. [see APARTHEID and NATIONALISM].

GARVEYISM: A movement [sometimes referred to as the "Back to Africa" movement] developed by Malcus Mosiah ("Marcus Aurelius") Garvey (1887-1940), a Jamaican-born nationalist and Pan-Africanist. Early on Garvey was a follower of Booker T. Washington (1856-1915). But over the years his philosophy was influenced by African nationalists, Pan-Africanists and African-American socialists. Central to this philosophy was the need to unite all Black people and to give them a racial self-confidence that would enable them to throw off white oppression. Garvey hoped to stimulate race pride both by direct propaganda and by the establishment of a powerful, independent Africa under the rule of Black men. To accomplish this goal he established a number of cultural and business "uplift" programs. Garvey's organizations were infiltrated by the FBI and accused of corruption. This resulted in his 1925 jailing on mail fraud charges and eventual deportation in 1927. Garvey continued organizing in Jamaica and Britain until his death in 1940. [see ETHIOPIANISM and AFRICA FOR THE AFRICANS]

HEGEMONY: In its basic definition hegemony simply means leadership or domination of one nation, state or class over another. The Italian Marxist, Antonio Gramsci (1891-1937), distinguished different forms of hegemony depending upon the historical situation and the classes involved. One aspect of hegemony dealt with the power of the state to "legally" force people to give their "spontaneous consent" to be ruled. This power can take a military,/ police, economic/political and a cultural form. [Example: if you are drafted into the military, you go or 1) you get arrested or court marshalled, 2) you are unable to apply for certain jobs or hold certain offices, or 3) you are branded a "draft-dodger/traitor" and looked down upon in your society/ culture.] State hegemony thus acts as a disciplinary force. *CULTURAL HEGEMONY* is where particular cultural forms (ruling class/ WASP) predominate over others (working class/minority), and the latter "accepts" this relationship of dominance. With regard to African-Americans, racism often plays a key role in the latter form of hegemony. Many of the problems which arose within the Pan-Africanist movement resulted from a basic contradictions: Pan-Africanism was both hegemonic and counterhegemonic.

IMPERIALISM: In general the term refers to the policies and practices of forming and maintaining an empire. There are, however, different theories of imperialism and why imperialist expansion takes place. Broadly speaking they can be divided into political theories (apologies for imperialism) and economic theories (criticisms of imperialism). Among the latter theorists was V.I. Lenin. According Lenin, imperialism is the "Highest stage of capitalism." It is characterized by the establishment of colonies, export of finance capital, control and exploitation of raw materials and world markets, and the subjugation of territories and their peoples. Lenin stresses that the

political (colonialism, neo-colonialism etc.) Since the end of the Second Imperialist World War, the United States has remained atop the imperialist heap, but is now being challenged by Japan and the European Common Market. [see also NEO-COLONIALISM]

MARXISM: Refers to the theories of SCIENTIFIC SOCIALISM developed by the German revolutionaries Karl Marx (1818-1883) and Frederik Engels (1820-1895) and the movements which developed from them. The two drew their philosophy from German classical philosophy, English political economy, utopian socialism, French Revolutionary politics and Russian anarchism. In their writings, Marx and Engels showed how the capitalist system exploits workers and the means of overcoming such exploitation through revolution. MARXISM-LENINISM [often used interchangeably with Marxism] refers to Lenin's contribution to Marx's theories. Lenin, the leader of the Russian Bolshevik Revolution, enriched Marxism in the era of imperialism and socialist revolution. He further developed Marx's theories of workers liberation, the dictatorship of the proletariat and the construction of a communist society. [see also SOCIALISM]

NATION OF ISLAM: A sect of Sunni Muslims begun by Wallace D. Fard in Detroit around 1930. Fard, who claimed to be from the holy city of Mecca, built an organization which he called the LOST-FOUND NATION OF ISLAM. His followers were mostly unemployed Black men from the south, angered by northern racism and the depression. In 1934, Fard mysteriously disappeared, and the leadership of his organization passed to his lieutenant Elijah Muhammad (1897-1975 — born Robert Poole in Sandersville, Ga.) upon his release from prison (for draft evasion) after W.W. II, who shifted his recruitment focus to the Black outcasts (pimps, hustlers, drug dealers etc.) of American society. Seeing their potential as converts he created

educational and social programs for ghetto youth and ex-convicts. By 1958 his membership had grown dramatically to nearly 15,000, with an estimated 50,000 sympathizers. His followers maintained a high moral standard and self-discipline, but there was little that was "revolutionary" (i.e. which challenged the system of oppression) in their actions. The Nation's early ideology only provided a means of affirming dignity and self-respect among it followers. This was to change with the recruitment of Malcolm Little to the group. Little, who took the name Malcolm X after his conversion, became minister of Harlem's Temple No. 7 in 1954. Thereafter he became the chief spokesperson for the Nation. Until he split with Elijah in 1964, Malcolm X built a large following of young Blacks through his militant nationalist (Garveyite) rhetoric. Malcolm's banishment from the Nation and subsequent assassination in 1965, left the organization divided. Even so, Elijah continued to lead the group until his death in 1975, when his son Wallace D. Muhammad took over. Within a few years Wallace transformed the Nation into an orthodox Islamic organization and renamed it the WORLD COMMUNITY OF AL-ISLAM IN THE WEST. However, disgruntled followers (led by Louis Farrakhan — Malcolm's successor as spokesperson) unhappy with the abandonment of Elijah's philosophy, reestablished the "old" Nation of Islam in 1981. Both organizations still exist today, although Farrakhan's is the more visible.

NATIONALISM: In general, Nationalism is a unifying belief that the interests of the nation (represented by the privileged class) and the people coincide — outweighing any other consideration. Although there are competing theories of nationalism, modern nationalism is a belief in (and the practice of) forming and maintaining a nation-state. Often implicit in nationalism are ideas of superiority (i.e. jingoistic patriotism/chauvinism

184

nationalism are ideas of superiority (i.e. jingoistic patriotism/chauvinism — the opposite of internationalism). In Western Europe, nation-states resulted from years of war and colonization. They first took shape after the breakdown of feudalism and the growth of capitalism in the 17th and 18th centuries. In the late 19th century AFRICAN NATIONALISM arose (particularly in West Africa). Its early stages stressed the belief that African territories (created by European conquest and colonialism) should be allowed to form independent nation-states. This was based on the European concept of nation-state as a political and economic entity, controlled by a ruling class [as opposed to African Socialism or internationalism.] In the diaspora of the 20th century, BLACK NATIONALISM emerged among African descendents in the Americas. Black Nationalists emphasized their ties to Africa and demanded that the continent (as a collection of nation-states) be independent. Black CULTURAL NATIONALISM, an offshoot of Black Nationalism, stressed the greatness of the African cultural heritage. Its primary focus is to validate African culture as a way of giving dignity to African-Americans [In the 1960's characterized by groups like United Slaves (US) and the Congress of African People (CAP).] Another form of Black Nationalism is REVOLUTIONARY NATIONALISM, a more militant (and less narrow) concept which has socialist and internationalist content. Revolutionary nationalism rejects the racist base of capitalist society and advocates self-determination and armed defense. [In the 1960's characterized by groups like the Black Panthers, Republic of New Africa (RNA), and the Revolutionary Action Movement (RAM).] Critics of revolutionary Black Nationalism often refer to it as LEFT-WING NATIONALISM (a reference to its narrowness).

NEGRITUDE: A movement begun by French-speaking African and Caribbean students rural in Jamaica during the 1930's. Its' followers believe that Ethiopian Emperor Haile Salassie (Ras Tafari) was a deity. They developed a subculture which is tied to Pan-Africanism, Ethiopianism and Garveyism [see above].

SELF-DETERMINATION: An anti-imperialist principle which calls for the right of communities to determine for themselves how they are run — i.e. without the interference or domination by foreign or domestic government officials. In the 1960's it became a rallying cry for Black Nationalists demanding community control of schools and an end to police brutality.

SOCIAL DARWINISM: The pseudo-scientific application of the British scientist Charles Darwins' (1809-1882) theory of evolution. The Social Darwinists, led by the English sociologist Herbert Spencer (1820-1903), carried Darwin's theory of "the survival of the fittest" into the field of human social relations. They believe that ruling classes were made up of "superior" (i.e. White) people who had won the "right" to rule over lesser (i.e. working class White and all "non-white") people. In essence, Social Darwinism was a form of racism/White chauvinism which has justified imperialist colonial expansion, exploitation of people of color, and race and class hatred. It is also counter-revolutionary. Social Darwinists believe that society is like an animal: the government is the head, whileworkers are the hands which must obey the head — a firm rejection of the ideas of revolution and democracy.

SOCIALISM: A theory and a movement which advocates that working men and women each share equally in the fruits of their labor. It sees public (society/community) ownership and operation of production and distribution

in society as better (i.e. less exploitative) than private (exclusive individual) ownership. There have been many movements to establish such a system. Although socialist ideas have existed for centuries, the first movement occurred in the 1830's with *UTOPIAN SOCIALISM*. Its leaders, Saint-Simon (1760-1825), Fourier (1772-1837) and Owen (1771-1858), were idealistic dreamers who wanted to found communes of workers, but who did not understand the material conditions of capitalism. Taking these conditions into account, Marx and Engels advocated *SCIENTIFIC SOCIALISM* which would overturn capitalist rule, and replaced it with worker rule (dictatorship of the proletariat). During the independence struggles in Africa, many leaders rejected capitalism and neo-colonialism as strategies for development. They were also uneasy with Euro-socialism. Hence many attempted to "Africanize" socialism by advocating what they termed *AFRICAN SOCIALISM* (in Tanzania it was called UJAMA; in Kenya HARAMBEE; in Zambia HUMANISM; in Nkrumah's Ghana CONSCIENCISM etc.) In its various forms African Socialists have focused on internal political and economic developments. But as yet have not been able to break the cycle of underdevelopment.

RACISM: A theory which holds that people belonging to one race are biologically and culturally superior to others not of that race. Racism includes negative assumptions or prejudgments (prejudice), exclusionary actions (discrimination) and conscious or unconscious hatred of others based on race. Racism can be manifested through individual acts, institutional standards, and/or values imbedded in society. Racism can take the form of white chauvinism, Social Darwinism or Eurocentrism.

BIBLIOGRAPHY

The purpose of this book is to
introduce readers to the idea of
Pan Africanism and to briefly
chart its long history.
A secondary aim (which I hope
was successful) is to stimulate
readers to find out more about
the topic. The following
bibliography is designed to aid
in that process.

AJALA, ADEKUNLE. PAN-AFRICANISM: EVOLUTION, PROGRESS AND PROSPECTS. LONDON: ANDRE DEUTSCHE,1973.

CARTEY, WILFRED AND KILSON, MARTIN. THE AFRICAN READER: INDEPENDENT AFRICA. NEW YORK: VINTAGE BOOK,1970.

CHAMBERS, BRADFORD. CHRONICLES OF BLACK PROTEST. NEW YORK:NEW AMERICAN LIBRARY, 1968.

DAVIS, STEPHEN M. APARTHEID'S REBELS. NEW HAVEN: YALE UNIVERSITY PRESS, 1987.

DENNIS, DENISE. BLACK HISTORY FOR BEGINNERS. NEW YORK:WRITERS AND READERS, 1984.

DU BOIS, W.E.B. THE WORLD AND AFRICA. NEW YORK: INTERNATIONAL PUBLISHERS, 1946.

ESEDEBE, P. OLISANWUCHE. PAN-AFRICANISM: THE IDEA AND THE MOVEMENT 1776-1963. WASHINGTON D.C.: HOWARD UNIVERSITY PRESS, 1982.

GEISS, I. THE PAN-AFRICANISM MOVEMENT. LONDON: METHEUN,1974.

GIDDINGS, PAULA. WHEN AND WHERE I ENTER: THE IMPACT OF BLACK WOMEN ON RACE AND SEX IN AMERICA. TORONTO AND NEW YORK: BANTAM BOOKS, 1988.

HARDING, VINCENT. THE OTHER AMERICAN REVOLUTION. LOS ANGELES: CENTER FOR AFRO-AMERICAN STUDIES, 1980.

HARDING, VINCENT. THERE IS A RIVER. NEW YORK: VINTAGE BOOKS, 1983.

HARRIS, JOSEPH E. GLOBAL DIMENSIONS OF THE AFRICAN DIASPORA. WASHINGTON D.C.: HOWARD UNIVERSITY PRESS, 1982.

HILL, ROBERT AND BAIR, BARBARA. MARCUS GARVEY: LIFE AND LESSONS. BERKELEY AND LOS ANGELES: UNIVERSITY OF CALIFORNIA PRESS, 1987.

HOOKS, BELL. AIN'T I A WOMAN. BOSTON: SOUTHEND PRESS, 1981.JULY, ROBERT. THE ORIGINS OF MODERN AFRICAN THOUGHT. NEW YORK:FREDERICK A. PRAEGER, 1967.

LANGLEY, J.A. PAN-AFRICANISM AND NATIONALISM IN WEST AFRICA 1900-1945. LONDON: OXFORD UNIVERSITY PRESS, 1973.

LEGUM, COLIN. PAN-AFRICANISM: A SHORT POLITICAL GUIDE. NEW YORK: FREDERICK A. PRAEGER, 1962.

LEMELLE, SIDNEY J. AND KELLEY, ROBIN D.G. PAN-AFRICANISM `REVISITED. LONDON: VERSO PRESS, FORTHCOMING 1992.

LINCOLN, C. ERIC. THE BLACK MUSLIMS IN AMERICA. BOSTON: BEACON PRESS, 1961

MALCOLM X, AND HALEY, ALEX. THE AUTOBIOGRAPHY OF MALCOLM X. NEW YORK: GROVE PRESS, 1965.

MARABLE, MANNING. RACE, REFORM AND REBELLION. JACKSON: UNIVERSITY OF MISSISSIPPI PRESS, 1991.

MARINE, GENE. THE BLACK PANTHERS. NEW YORK: NEW AMERICAN LIBRARY, 1969.

M'BUYINGA, ELENGA. PAN-AFRICANISM OR NEO-COLONIALISM. LONDON: ZED PRESS, 1982.

MOSES, W.J. THE GOLDEN AGE OF BLACK NATIONALISM: 1850-1925. NEW YORK AND LONDON: OXFORD UNIVERSITY PRESS, 1978.

NKRUMAH, KWAME. AFRICA MUST UNITE. NEW YORK: INTERNATIONAL PUBLISHERS, 1979.

PADMORE, GEORGE. PAN-AFRICANISM OR COMMUNISM. NEW YORK: DOUBLEDAY ANCHOR BOOKS, 1971.

PARSONS, NEIL. A NEW HISTORY OF SOUTHERN AFRICA. LONDON: MACMILLAN PUBLISHERS, 1982.

ROBINSON, CEDRIC J. BLACK MARXISM: THE MAKING OF THE BLACK RADICAL TRADITION. LONDON: ZED PRESS, 1991.

THOMPSON, V.B. AFRICA AND UNITY: THE EVOLUTION OF PAN-AFRICANISM. LONDON: LONGMANS, 1969.

WILLIAMS, LORRAINE A. AFRICA AND THE AFRO-AMERICAN EXPERIENCE.WASHINGTON D.C.: HOWARD UNIVERSITY PRESS, 1977.